SAINTS + SINNERS

2021 and 2022
NEW POETRY
FROM THE FESTIVAL

SAINTS + SINNERS

2021 and 2022
NEW POETRY
FROM THE FESTIVAL

with introductions by our judges
Jewelle Gomez and Julie R. Enszer

edited by
Brad Richard and Paul J. Willis

Saints+Sinners
2022

Published in the United States of America by
REBEL SATORI PRESS
rebelsatori.com

SAINTS + SINNERS 2021 and 2022 NEW POETRY FROM
THE FESTIVAL

ISBN: 978-1-60864-049-2

Credits
Editors: Brad Richard and Paul J. Willis
Production Design: Brad Richard
Production Assistance: Tracy Cunningham
Cover Art by Timothy Cummings
Cover Design by Toan Nguyen
Book Design by Sven Davisson

Contents

2022 Poems on the Theme of Rain

2021 Poems on the Theme of Love

ACKNOWLEDGMENTS

We would like to thank:

The John Burton Harter Foundation for their continued generous support of the Saints and Sinners Literary Festival.

Susanne Sovern, Scovern Law Firm for generously underwriting our poetry contests.

Timothy Cummings, cover artist for the 2021 and 2022 Saints and Sinners Literary Festival poetry anthology and program books.

Everyone who has entered the contest and/or attended the Saints and Sinners Literary Festival over the last 19 years for their energy, ideas, and dedication in keeping the written LGBTQ word alive.

We'd also like to thank our 2021 participants, members, and sponsors for their understanding and support this past March when the pandemic forced us to host the entire Festival online, resulting in a beautiful Virtual Festival.

SAINTS + SINNERS

2022
NEW POETRY
FROM THE FESTIVAL
poems on the theme of rain

edited by
Brad Richard and Paul J. Willis

2022 Judge's Introduction

Julie R. Enszer

What a glorious pleasure to read these finalists for the Saints & Sinners Poetry Contest! It is always thrilling to see the quality of work queer poets are producing today. We write with a vast vision of our place in the world and of the value of queerness in reflecting, altering, and reimagining our world anew.

Michael Montlack's "Phantom Rain" immediately struck me with the arresting opening stanza, "Who mourns the droplets / that sublime before landing?" Generally as a reader, I encounter sublime as an adjective but here Montlack draws on chemistry to remind us that sublime is also when something turns to vapor with heat. Then that transgressive second question, "should we mourn?" Montlack is a poet working with all the power of language, the line, time, and memory. The concluding lines slayed me in the best way. I will return to this poem often.

I judged the poems without knowing the poets, but when the names were revealed, I smiled: familiar names—and new names. The collection gives me the sense of our fierce continuance in spite of the challenges around us.

I encountered this work anonymously in the midst of rereading Adrienne Rich for another writing project; I returned to "The Wreck" many times, both seduced by its smart engagements with Rich and by its defiance of Rich. Where Rich chose "to walk here. And draw this circle," Jeffrey Perkins asserts the desire to "remake years," "to walk / outside what we made." The dialogue with Rich is

1

lovely; the interlacing of rain, artful.

"The Cost" by Noel Quiñones is another poem in the batch of excellent rain poems to which I returned repeatedly while reading finalists. These powerful couplets gather meaning as they lay one atop the other finally asserting "all queerness comes at a cost" but there is "this little healing you've built in me, this little cause for love."

Reader, I commend all these poems to you. I am sure you will find poems that speak to you; I suspect you will quibble with my decisions. I delight in that, as I hope you will delight in reading this work then searching out more by these extraordinary poets.

Editor's Note

I just came in from the rain. Light February rain, not enough to keep me out of my garden this morning, a pleasant drizzle as I hauled mulch in a wheelbarrow, rolling it from a heap by the compost pile to the edges of new beds and paths I've been working on all winter. Slow work, work I'm grateful to be doing, grateful for what it brings, for all the ways it feeds me. And I'm grateful for the slowness of this rain—as if it's meditating on what it means to rain and to be rain, which reminds me to be mindful of my work, the what and why of it.

Given New Orleans's precarious relationship with weather, I'm grateful that I can garden in the winter. In the hot half of the year, we're on constant alert for so-called Rain Events, which range from massive thunderstorms to full-blown tropical storms and hurricanes, all super-charged by global warming, each one blurring land into water a little more. If you've lived here a while, you say you're used to it, but we live with a collective anxiety that's as heavy and pervasive as the humidity. It's literally the air we breathe.

The cooler half of the year feels lighter in every sense. An autumn dry spell feels downright luxurious, a gift. Cold winter rain—rarely a deluge, often as gentle as the rain I gardened in this morning—and low winter clouds make our gray-green landscapes faintly gleam, the perfect backdrop for camellias and early-blooming magnolias. You forget the fears summer storms bring; you remember other winters; you dream. And then there's spring, when a sudden storm can leave the late afternoon light astoundingly clear, the colors of the sky and the city speaking vividly to one another. Those are the times when we remember to be grateful for the rain.

Right now, I'm grateful for all these poems about rain. What struck me most in reading the submissions, but particularly our finalists' poems, is how strongly rain inclines us to introspection, especially about relationships: romantic relationships, friendships, our relationships to place and self, all of these always changing, the way rain changes the world around us and our relationship to it.

3

Not surprisingly, rainy days are often good writing days. I'm betting many of the amazing poems you're about to read were rainy day work. I hope you'll read and re-read them. Keep them handy for—you guessed it—a rainy day. And forgive, please, me for taking this opportunity to share a rain poem of my own:

Brad Richard
Board Member, The Tennessee Williams & New Orleans Literary Festival
Chair, Saints and Sinners Festival Advisory Committee

4

The Rain

—for Tim

I need you to remember the rain—
   lie down with me, love, and remember
      all the rain we know, while we know;

how it talked to itself through afternoons
   like a boy with his imaginary playmate,
      rain lost to itself in its coming, as we listened;

how its burst down morning lawns
   ended bright-beaded on castor-bean leaves
      and in your hair when you came in with the dog;

how the hurricane pelted through the porch screen,
   as we sat naked there in the after-dark, heat
      heavy with wet, our slick skin one with night;

how sudden a fall—imagine you and me
   loosened from the sky, oblate,
      pancake-shaped, small wobbling

spheres cast down and finding
   in falling one another, falling in air
      as in one another, how, one body

spirited homeward, heavier
   in falling further, we're swallowed
      in earth's mouths.

Michael Montlack

Winner of the 2022 Saints and Sinners Poetry Contest

Phantom Rain

Who mourns the droplets
that sublime before landing?

And should we mourn?

Why not relish their freefall.
Envying the thrill, the speed
uninterrupted by impact.

Maybe they are the blessed.
Part acrobat, part magician.
Evaporation a superpower.

Maybe they spare the Earth
an over-battering or floods.
Nature's quiet martyrs.

My friend Barbara passed
in her sleep suddenly. Mystified,
her twin continues to plummet.

Where did she go? she asks.

All I can do is take her hand
as we fall together. Remembering

those perfect smoke rings
Barbara blew as a teenager.

How we begged her. *Teach us!*

The beauty of those rings
elongating and disappearing.
I can still smell them.

Earthy. Musky. Not unlike
petrichor moments after
the downpour has ceased.

The Fierceness of Rainbows

For Buddhists, the highest state achievable
before attaining Nirvana is the *rainbow body*.

In Greek mythology, Iris rides a rainbow
to bring humanity messages from the Gods.

After Noah saved the animals from the flood,
God sent one to say, *It won't happen again.*

Indra, the Hindu God of thunder and war,
used a rainbow to shoot arrows of lightning.

In Burma the Karens believe the rainbow
to be painted demons that eat children.

Amazonian cultures blame it for miscarriages.

While the Cherokee say it's the hem of the sun's coat.

Star-crossed lovers in an old Chinese folktale
must wait for a rainbow to be alone together.

In Norse religion, a burning rainbow bridge
connects Earth with the home of the Gods.

Some Shamans in Siberia think rainbows
the way to ascend to the sky-spirit realm.

According to Australian Aboriginal tribes,
the Rainbow Serpent created the world.

We all know about the feisty Leprechaun ...

And today—in any culture, anywhere—
it's the fierce pride of the queer spectrum.

Ezra Adamo

We, spiteful bodies:

I want, like balm, to be
the kind of bitch (affectionate)

who reads *Spring and All*
during Spring; that equinox,
opened, blanched:

veiled rain through
70's camera angles;
heavy linen breeze
holds skin.

The cover is blue, robin's
egg shell soft, not spotted.

Sweeter than always, he—
sing—before I know him;

we'll roll blueberries
into our mouths, baseline,
surround fingertips.

We, the word, a beacon;
need quieter bodies.

eighteen and before:

//

poems with imaginary men
   (maybe not so)—
      blue-borne figures;

curl your body behind me—
there could be a sweeter
coat on my tongue;

termite bites lounge
to heal—crust up
knuckles;

sculpture-ethereal—
i wish i were clay or paint,

like everybody does—

there isn't enough water
here—

my scars are strike paper,
powdered red phosphorus—

need rain, matches, or maybe

maybe maybe

cis men's fingers
(morbid
trans validation

Carafe

When i am bones,
myrtle tree branches,
my ribs can be shelves
for green flowers and
shed cat whiskers
and and

placed in any rain
for opossums to sleep;

Scott Bailey

Rorschach Pasture

    Sipping chamomile tea to calm the tyranny of ambition,
the duvet neatly folded down to reveal red satin sheets
  cool as watermelons in the summer heat, I'm half asleep
in my Queen Ann chair when my mother calls to tell me
  about a racket behind the house, so I slowly dress
to walk the fence line, flash-lighting the night pasture,
    eventually entering the gate near the creek enriching
the fruit of kumquat trees under which I say, "Delinquents
  come forth," & three calves walk my way, the leg
of one entangled in chicken wire, a termite-infested
  post in tow, yards of snagging wire like a trailing hem
of calves unaware of the hunger, on the hill, stalking them
  thrilled to see me, the encumbered calf accidentally
kicking then licking me, a bittersweet sensation which
    triggers a memory of one day after school when I
stretched out among a spreading bed of baby's breath
  near sandstones in the pasture, pretending to be dead,
evidently my scorned effeminacy an insufficient stench,
  buzzards circling a mile above me less than a minute,
but seemingly an eternity, a chainsaw quartet in the distance,

  when swallows attacked a swarm of bees fleeing felled trees,
the sawdust sky a Rorschach deck of bees shifting formation:
  I saw a hand reaching down for me below clouds so near,
my soul like a trough pouring over during storms.
  "Better to have bored buzzards & bullies calling you queer,
than a pack of wolves unsatisfied by a scrawny deer,"
  I tell the unweaned calves led to heifers worrying cud
in the barn with its door ajar, the loose hinge secured

before heading to the sandstones still there where I
    sit in darkness beneath a crescent moon, waiting for eyes
like stars to creep from the shadows of pines
    like lean, dancing men when a fearsome wind ushers
in a howl of all howls followed by lightning striking
    a pine split in two, flare-like embers singeing the backsides
of what I thought to be a pack of wolves actually
    a posse of possums heard hissing well beyond my pasture,
thunder trembling the ground I swoon upon, dizzy with laughter.

First published by the *Jabberwock Review*

Divine Reversal

Driving from the lake where I broke bread with tadpoles

& minnows among shadows of swamp grass, I see a doe

knee-deep in red clover on the road's shoulder, so

I slow down to photo burst the crimson crowns in her dewy eyes,

but her head turns toward the thicket of orange trumpet vines

laid claim to what remains of a fence, her ears perked, as if

expecting love to follow her through despite the itchy

leaves. ——— & when she vanishes, as if she leaped into the

blinding sun in the rearview mirror, I recall a dream:

I am searching for my boyfriend in a fiery field. I hear him

calling my name, his fading voice leading me to a church parking

lot where I am left behind, holding his hymnal darkened

by ash, a dream that can wring the joy from a Ferris-wheel

day, the psyche a temple of delight where melancholy builds

her shrine, but this day, thus far, remains unclaimed, my dear Keats.

Half a mile away, I see a fawn playing chase with a beagle

puppy in a yard, so I stop to livestream the fawn awkwardly

bending down with her stilt-like legs to sniff the puppy barking

at my idled car, the fawn unsure of what to do in this world

of amused abandonment, her wagging tail a clue she's unafraid

when her future self has reason to. I almost pull into the driveway

to knock on a stranger's door to share this extraordinary

beauty, if unaware, but I continue on North Dexter road,

the light, in me, less dim: that fawn & puppy a rainbow

on this tearful day, hours after planting lilies at his grave.

What Walking Brings

Dear reader, how do you handle despair?
I have wept under a weeping willow
  where I prayed for one eye, mourned the other beyond repair.
Imagine the only window
  boarded up: a nightmare no one should have nor bear.
    I need not imagine a fist nor oily grit
of gay-bar parking lot, nor the humility
  of living with parents to afford surgeries in Mississippi
where I have seen desperation in a gas station
  checkout line: a man shoplifting Vienna sausages
to buy a Colt 45, a poor drunkard's breakfast.
    I have imagined a limb for a limb, old law satisfaction,
when mourning a treetop the power crew
  cut down. All for nought, I thought, bemoaning
a downgraded cyclone,
  yet praising the lovely disaster of pine needles strewn
about roads before spraying plum trees festooned
  with worms writhing within tents of silk, a pestilence
for sure, but a world of joy for a boy wielding a stick.
    I have walked on Mississippi's Sargasso Sea,
kudzu flowing like the mighty Mississippi,
  kudzu hogging sunlight from fields once corn & sugarcane,
crops forgotten, fields unmaintained.
    I have misplaced my optimism on a creek bank,
or did I
  lend it to the man I sideswiped on the meat aisle,
a man I loved gone to love a plumber in Dover,
  Delaware, nowhere near my reflection changed by tadpoles
& a maple leaf I followed downstream,
  a leaf later held between seen & unseen streams
spinning a leaf in its place of wisdom:
  Breathe with me awhile, the leaf whispered.
    The nearby blackberry bushes picked clean,

I have called in sick to walk in the rain,
 a youthful delight of many returns:
like the simplicity of pork-rind currency
 & mud-pie bake sales on pond banks: a time
that lingers ——— like my fear of going blind.
 If my left eye goes, I must walk that road.
 "   A worthy idleness seeks Beauty & Grace,"
I should have told the alcoholic looting a vacuum machine,
 slinging a hose against pavement
only to dislodge gum in a whiskey receipt, or so
 I thought, until a daddy longlegs fled the hose.
 If I am a part of all I have met, my dear Lord Tennyson,
what am I to learn from the man
 who glued then screwed a Mercedes-Benz
ornament to a Chevrolet Nova's hood mangled
 by a deer, antlers stuck in the grill? Am I a man
allowing pride & loss to guide me so long as I exist?
 I have stared into the soapy abyss
of a crockpot until I heard God: Once you sew that fist
 in that quilt, will you close that door & let me in?
I said, "Yes," yet I still dwell on my misgivings
 & my regrets. ——— I admire straw fires that ignite
as fast as they die out, a burn that does not linger unlike
 my fear of going blind. If my left eye goes, I must walk that road.
 Have you watched the sunset through bullet holes
of a cattle-crossing sign? Thrown an engagement
 ring that rolled after someone on the stairs? Relationships
outweigh solitude, allegedly,
 nonetheless, happiness or despair either way,
a joyous or wretched river in us, a sea all about us,
 a cliché within a cliché, my dear Eliot:
better to wade in hope than drown in misery.
 I could allow briars in my fig tree
or jog the valley to greet the breeze atop my hill
 where I have watched swallows feeding
above the dust of bush-hogged fields.

Why not ignore the sign, Bridge Out Ahead?
Even dead ends lead somewhere:
  I found an armchair once, so I ate a pear, I read
Baudelaire. J'adore the taken elsewhere.
        I love to count the leaves that waltz across the streets.
Have you noticed such peace?
  Although I admire the graceful rage of asphalt pavers
so stern each day, I prefer the minnow
  that quakes the lake, the bug that skates such waves.
Then there's the crane that stands in the shallows
  along the bank, hours on end, if need'th be, so still
        unlike the sun crowning my hill
where I have knelt, where I kneel
  to consider my fields, ——— my soul among tilled rows,
walking where irises shall grow.

Stacey Balkun

For Maggie

I dedicate the strawberry moon
to making blackberry pie.
I think all you had said was *hi*

and I came running, high
off the wet summer grass.

Your car wouldn't start, the key
stuck in the ignition, unturned.
You cut my bangs on the back porch,

sitting so close our knees banged
and we let the mosquitos have at it

for hours, didn't even notice
the darkness of the new moon.
It had rained a week straight,

the thunder driving me straight to you.
And so still a fool, I stood up,

drove east to get lost in a patch
of blackberries and canning recipes.
I forgot to set my intentions.

I forgot to pick up pectin.
Lately, everything turns me on,

fucking everything, even tablespoons.

My fingers calloused from failing
to fix your engine,

my arms so scratched from thorns,
I try not to keep picking

up the silent phone.
I pray you keep sending pictures.
I pray the next time you turn

a key, something opens.
How full the moon now, unlocking

the dark, berry-stained sky.
How foolish when I realize
my intention all along was you.

After the Rain

and after the floods, she tells me
the river is a monster

because it continues to cut
away the land

without pulling her house
any closer to mine.

Aubade with Farmhouse

after Kay Sage's painting In the Third Sleep *(1944)*

I sail through morning aloft, buoyed
by a strange light. You appeared
in half of my thousand dreams.

The wide porch smells like raw hops,
like the mud in the chicken pen after a rain.
I watch my dry hands reach for a chipped mug

of black coffee. Where have you gone?
I pick at my nail beds. The birds screech.

Aubade with Tornado Watch

after Kay Sage's painting Tomorrow, Mister Silver *(1949),*
with a line from Rachel Eliza Griffiths

when the forecast says *all clear*
it doesn't mean everywhere

I mean I tried building this ship from bones
but the bay is empty   crusted with salt

I mean, this is the experience of hunger
my ribs exposed
               I tried

to hoist a flag   *in the middle*
of a city   *I am*

between years of   *ruin*
shadow all derelict and debris

I mean it was like being a wife
and I didn't like it

      of course I looked back

I haven't felt the sun in months,
my rainboots crusted with mold

and still, sandbags
to gather   storm drains

to plumb and once I've picked up
every torn scrap of tarp, more

will blow through   *between storms*
I have learned   still does not mean *calmed*

Danielle Bero

Wet:Dry:Mud

Wet

candid lilies speckled white
rising above sea level
into the eyes and ears of children
and doves released at weddings
throwing rice
                    and limbs
adding spice to hymns
the water creeps into windows
falls off the roofs

we submerge ripped petals floating to the top
w/ lilies for hands
to swat bees as they pollinate the air
w/ our new sex

we can't drown here
we are too special to die wet and soggy

Dry

flowers blooming with no eyes to watch
petals fall to bare cement
pollen floating through the quiet streets
blowing into gutters and sewer drains
flowing into sky
a run-on sentence of pinks and yellows

human bodies bone dry
ripple and wave
watering the Earth's dirt with our sweat

we succumb to the floor
to bass drum gods no pills no touching
in this church of alone in the dark
moving to space hymns
reaching for sound
while visions of holy ghosts reach for the aux
bouncers checking pulses
muffled beats pumping from inside
the heart/ the DJ- skipping

we are all sick now
fever vibrating/ snot flowing
warm to the touch but no one to check
our foreheads with the backs of hands

boom cat scat for the culture
boom boom cat to scare off the vultures
swooping, they circle and peck
but we are not dead yet

Mud

just glitter specks
swirling in space
latching on and bouncing off
live carcasses dancing in all black
like the browning cherry blossoms
dropping on to desolate ground
that's been watered with our bodies
the fruit of this planet
spoiling in the sun

w/ seeds to spread and grow
waiting to be picked off
link arms and souls in protest
so we are harder to scavenge
b/c we are sick
but not dead yet

My Storia

Dedicated to Astoria, Queens

Slurp the water from the hydrant,
spraying out of a double opened soup can
and project it over the monkey bars
splashing hyper-colored shirts
into orange and pink
acid washed jeans
        scrunched up around
        emerging calf muscles

Streetlights flicked on as the dinner call
mom let the Led out of a record

pasta with homemade sauce
tomatoes from the backyard
dad picked the seeds out for me
sprinkled a little dill, salt, pepper
with a glass of whole milk
in a washed-out jelly jar

His weed smoke limboed under my
bedroom door, I scribbled with gel pens

        The sticky summers
        of collecting cicada skins
        and writing my name in
smashed lightning bug butts

They never questioned when I pulled
cargo shorts out of my brother's drawer
to sag just enough to see My Little Pony panties

I dug a pool in the back where lightning uprooted a tree
and laid plastic wrap over the hole
to hold water
        They just snapped Fuji pics of me with
the shovel for scrapbooks

I'm a ½ product
of sidewalks and processed foods

falling asleep to mom reading *Where
the Sidewalk Ends*

Poems to tell Nanny I miss her and she should
not have smoked cigarettes anyway
they let me throw a letter tied to a rock
into the sky for hours trying to reach heaven

Son of a Butch

I am woman as a vessel
a design trapped over soul
to Bryson Tiller women of interest
    I am the tropics
        the thunder
            the Aries inside your love
Sun and daughter   not quite mother
Rough tender the lion and the lamb
        a kebob of predator and victim

I am 35 and 14 angsty
a strong believer in education with imagination
    rethinking the brick building, paperwork sheets and the
    school lunch trays
my spirit will always be the   NYC skyline
I know every line to *The Matrix*, we lie in slimy sacs dozing in and
    out
    of protest and complacency
I'm like a sun shower in all its dichotomy bright and chilling in my
    duplicity
I am not American cheese   brick by brick half melting

I am basically 40 years old
I am a strong believer in Jhene Aiko
swirling sound bowls from LA epicenters
My spirit will always be the NY city skyline then, now and forever
    to come
under water   inside fire
I know every line to the *Fridays*
even on a Monday
I'm like glitter in cement sparkling under fresh J's
I am not afraid of war   I am ready   maybe
les be real, prolly not ready for war but

I put black paint under my eyes
Left Eye to be exact
  b/c I am a strong believer in that TLC, Aaliyah and all the
  other fallen black women soldiers
I hold up in my room late at night
         blunt and posters
my spirit will always be covered
  in rainbow prisms
I know every line to poems written by middle schoolers in Title 1
  forgotten city
backstreets
I write their lines inside my palms and sweat them off before it is
  time to recite

I am, I am

Dragging the bottom of my pants from East River
to Lake Toba to Lake Tahoe
I put me over rice
You place me on the rocks
  I am would you rather.

Slouched Sock Seeds

I aint a punk
       but at night I squish
my eyes
to avoid sounds

the knock on my door
       I recoil into a soup
       diced and soft
           & nice for an
               upset tummy

  a woman alone
nothing more than a punk
       not enough
salt from tears
       to season
the seasons changing
       the cause
           of some tears
I migrate west
           then back east
now south
           what feels so righteously southern
to sunbake, picking off locusts

home is in my sneakers
like there is no way out
       slouched socks
       to dap heels
and say life is just a series of Q and A
the answer might be *we aint no punks*
we just plant broken and cracked seeds anyway just in case
    something sprouts

we sing to them as the journey w/ words for therapy

I pull my fuckin socks back up
& synch my anks
      tether to the streets
           to remind the
rest of you
I have no bark or bite
      just bones and sick days
and unread emails
and exes I can still smell in my blankets I set fire to
slow burn that shit
        & fuck them anyway
I'm no punk ass bitch
regardless
      of what you heard, or read on the internet, or saw
I flex sometimes
      I buck
& foam at the mouth
just to water the cracked seeds
      pleading for them to grow something
          buncha punk asses anyway

Jeremy Halinen

Loowit Ape Caves, Lower Cave

It's about to rain,
he said,

ending
our long

silence.
We were half

a mile
past the entrance;

the only light
we could see

was unnatural,
its source

a headlamp
third eyeing

away from us
about to vanish

beyond the bend
in the lava tube

it was illuminating
for eyes

not its own.
For nearly

an hour
we'd been sitting

wrapped
in damp blankets

on a rough
cold stone

about a yard
from the slime

on the wall,
our headlamps

switched off,
intermittently

interrupted
darkness

dilating
our pupils,

my head
at huddle

on his shoulder.
He hadn't meant

more drips
from cave-side

36

and -ceiling
stalactites

but all
tenebrific

clouds
I'd ever seen

fomenting
a storm

aloft
my eyes

with one
I hadn't.

Fourth Chakra

Dahlias are dying. Even airplanes
are flying south. All yesterday
air was full of broken
hearts disguised as raindrops. The maples
aren't bare yet but undressing,
dressing earth, soil
soggy underfoot.

Spiders patrol willowy webs in silence
while beneath them squirrels
nibble acorns in peace.

I am headed south into a breeze,
toward the water tower
and a towering cedar.
Calls of crows circling the oaks
release unease from my heart,
scavenge my disease. I will go home soon.
I will go home
to you healed.

Lepidoptera Metamorphosis

for Katherine Stribling

Though you went underwater
to hear Orion's Belt smolder,

you saw sky teeth waver.
Torn between shore and ocean,

your pockets heavy with stones.
Morrow eve, by the river's mouth.

Soon you may be rain.
Skin veils you in vain.

An eclipse of dragon moths
trying to divorce the moon

from her reflection.

Casket

for Marie Laveau

You're going to need a friend outside.
Your friend will need a hatchet,

a stone, and a book of matches
to burn your bones with the casket.

Your friend will fashion a crow
from the stone with her hatchet.

You will enter that crow
and turn it to feather and bone.

Fly to him at new moon.
When the moon is newest, sharpen your claws.

Go for the throat when he opens his eyes.
Don't let go until his nest is drenched.

Rest the rest of the night on his wings.
Let the stars calm your dreams.

At dawn, wake refreshed and clean the nest.
Fly to the nearest river; drink your fill.

Come nightfall, bury him in your empty grave.
Make sure to bury every feather.

Sleep the rest of the night in his nest.
When you wake, burn the nest and dried blood.

Carry a coal in your claw to his grave.

Dig him up and smolder his bones.

His feathers will be flames in moments.
His wings will never fly again.

Be careful not to breathe the smoke.
When the fire has gone out, find his claws.

Fly them back to the burned nest.
Bind the claws together and bury them in ash.

After the next rain, retrieve his claws.
Drop them anywhere in the river.

When they sink, fly downstream.
When you reach the fifth bend, build a nest.

Sing a new song from your new beak.
Day will break and break again.

Your dreams will come and go like stones
carved into the shapes of crows.

The river will erase his claws.
You'll be more flesh than stone.

Jamie Kim-Worthington

dictionary rain

rain [reyn]
noun
  1. milk teeth. the city i'm in has people who carry their
     happiness like a frail animal and people who carry their
     sadness into the rain to strip it away. the sorrows turn gray,
     milky, then dissolve. the metal sheen of buildings glimmers
     like milk teeth.
  2. it's raining again. i want to be a better person but it's raining
     again.
  3. i rinse colanders of blackberries to the white-noise sound of
     the rain flowing down my window. water inside and out, on
     my hands and on my balcony. to find beauty in blackberry
     seeds and tap water is a lovely and strenuous thing.
  4. my bones are hostels and my hair is dripping onto the
     carpet. if this body were not my own, maybe i would find
     it beautiful. if this body were made of rain and the rain-
     feelings that accompany it. maybe then.

Ophelia lies submerged in the river as raindrops tap the surface

The drowning was not pleasant—
Fingers pruny, knuckles white
And beads of saliva trickling from my mouth into my eye
As I hang from a tree washed up ashore
Bent at such an angle
That allows it to fall into my tears.
You know the sort—
Think of a drowned woman, and Ophelia comes to mind.

I am the strange,
The canopy bed floating down the river, pristine and upright,
And the screams that press against the lungs, making them burst.
There's delicacy in my features
The same way that there's beauty in a wolf,
Or the bones of a crow,
Or eggshell fragments.

I lie under the surface tension of the river
and watch the raindrops circulate over the skin of the water.
I lie under the river and watch as rain drives the floodbanks up.
I lie under the water and pray.

Pray you, love, remember.
Remember my limbs the same way I remember
How the light shimmers from above the river water
As my head drifts downwards towards the bed.
Remember the pansies and rosemary i vomit,
Spilling over my lips and coating my cheeks
And remember that I will be back soon.

Jeffrey Perkins

How I Miss the Rain

> "Rain finally came + it's beautifully cool."
> —John Cage in a letter to Merce Cunningham, postmarked June
> 29, 1943

Last night it poured, like last year
when John and Brice visited—
a very East Coast kind of rain,

fully committed. And now, the sun
is too late for anything except a tease.
Can it be enough to end a drought?

Back East too much snow for anyone
but it does make a good excuse for
a nap. They can finally light their fires.

"…my first feeling about the rain
was that it was like you." How it built
from nothing but a glance on a boat.

You loved to find a reason to go back
to bed so I took a nap on my rough couch
as penance for not sharing one with you.

You told me the one thing I couldn't
say after I left was that I missed you.

Climb Through the Mountain

We're in uncharted territory. It's raining in LA.
Raining behind the walls of my casita painted red.

Drinking mezcal and remembering bikes up the hill
by the schoolhouse in the seaside town where we met.

Sometimes you can go back by remembering the feel
of your feet in sandals. The taste of the rum punch.

The blue of the bay off the deck. Friends. I remember
the Dostoevsky on my bedside table and your nose.

What can I get away with—with words? What love
and tricks? I spent a month learning to sing

to a shadow. When I say something now I know
you've been here before and you'll be back.

All the poems you're meant to read are here.
Fragments of your future you can feel inside.

Promise when you hear a brook you'll think of this
raining night. The sound of water on stone.

Wash whatever you need to be free of. What happened
to the performance the dancer was set to perform?

Canceled before he could go on. Imagine
that level of dedication, just to lose it in the end.

The Wreck
Runner-Up, 2022 Saints and Sinners Poetry Contest

Rain drenched the afternoon
and this morning the sun drilled in.

I've watched this day change its mind
about you and me. Happy Birthday.

What drew me to you was your love
of that Adrienne Rich poem—

the love for the wreck and not the story.
Our mutual desire for annihilation

and maybe an intoxicating admiration
of what we are both missing.

A wish to remake years. To walk
outside what we made and into else.

The desire for rain when it's bright and
sun when the bleakness invades.

These Thoughts

This thought about my eventual death
does not mean anything. This thought
about my family's history with love does
not mean anything. My thought about
lost lovers does not mean anything.
This thought about doubt and holding
it together, does not mean anything.
This thought about perfect novels and
James Baldwin does not mean anything.
My love for Latrice does not mean anything.
This thought about rain in Los Angeles
and my complicated relationship with it
doesn't mean anything. My wish for sun
and no consequences. This thought about
capitalism manipulating desire into death
does not mean anything. This thought
about my credit score. This desire for sex
and not wanting it does not mean anything.
This thought about civil disobedience
does not mean anything. This thought
about missing you and all my thoughts
about you do not mean anything. The last
photo I took of you at Mogador. Our last
morning. Your look across the table. This
thought about endings.

Noel Quiñones

Runner-Up, 2022 Saints and Sinners Poetry Contest

The Cost

for Edyka

The violet warning of a San Antonio sky is more than I can fathom.
May 5th an offering to idols as we talk desert talk, hybrids in the
    last city

daring to dance at language's edge. You tell me Spirit considers you
a river and we don't pray for dams as often as we pray for rain.

Your eyes, two quilted burdens, recount how a body's knowing
can paralyze a woman so close to god even her mouth poses:

an O, as willing and unwilling balance themselves toward grace.
What terrible sanctuaries we have come to call home. Hermana

my lips matched the morning, and I wept with the mirror's soft
answer. I told my last and only love not to come back until
    sunrise—

so often I wonder myself, just a few bones barren of a path,
if I can call my body a complex animal and mean it. Purple

are my crescent knees, waking toward Sunday's judge.
As the transient witness to my own levees, I lay

belly up in la aguamiel, as you offer nature's promise:
all queerness comes at a cost and I don't know what you mean

until I do. The search for my original name shaded by yours,
this little healing you've built in me, this little cause for love.

Jen Rouse

It Will All Rain

I.

Maybe the portraits. Dark curls at cords of the neck, close. Candela-
bra. Holy smoke blowing across the bed. Roses of the dead at your
lips. I kept the air for you. Watching your messages transfer from
hawk to leaf to palm. And palm to kiss. Where you sit for all my
days and drifting nights. This time. And next. And next again. Not a
spell. Not in the way they mean now. The witches who do not know
that what comes next is what remains from a time they never knew.
But I do. Remember the ways of passing each breath, here, now and
between us. Come. The way you remember all my words. Woman
began in my mouth. Not so long ago. And so long ago. You are small
to me here. Where we are cold. And the drapes are drawn.

Knocknarea Hill, County Sligo

Just there in the woods. The silky fuzz of your newly shorn head
against my breast. So young and smitten. You followed me to the
top. And that night, after the bar, so proud, called your fiancée from
a phone booth to say: *Maybe her. Just her. Her name?* a whisper.

Ghost girl. Intoxicating. Wild. And the wind on the hill drags at
your heels, back. Home. I am queen and queen again. Open into the
cry of the lambs on the sea side. We stumble down. Skin knees and
cling to burn in the salt and surf. Let me show you how to hold the
weight of me. Listen when I tell you: *choose one stone.*

II.

Followed the years of armor. A mesh of sword and anger heft. You met me in every parking lot. Always: *What do you imagine will happen between us?* I lit your Salem. I licked the menthol from your lips. Maybe you held us there, two women on a mountain. Dangerous with swans and poems. But I was so much: *When all is ruin once again.*[1] You were soft and captured laughter. So many times I begged you to leave. So many times you stood in my light.

III.   Ames, IA

When he said, *I know, I love her too.* I learned
the art of living from the middle. The constant
cowardice of others. And leaving alone.

IV.

Betrayal and belief will find
you on a grey leather
couch staring down
an aging psychologist, letting
her finger trail your cheek.
Then those long lunches
at the gallery. The Rothko.
The last time when she said,
I didn't realize how beautiful.
                    How damned.
And then a burgundy couch.
And then a couch in garish florals.
And finally a couch, impenetrable
and her dead husband
in the corner of the room,
constantly glaring at you.

---

1   Thoor Ballylee Tower plaque, W.B. Yeats.

V.   Iowa City, IA

Then, there's an ER, alone. Because no matter
how many times you show up, no one
ever accompanies you. Maybe your expectations
are as high as the manic kite you fly. Maybe when
you crumble again, you'll choose not to
eat the crumbs. Choose not to eat their crumbs.

VI.   Homeland

When you don't sleep for days,
you watch Claire Danes pretend
to bipolar cry. And she tells you,
with a coy side eye, here, this
is what I do:
                    First admit.
It will all rain down upon you
like the crazy it is. Be ready.
Wipe the lens, and slowly knit
your brows in a most deliberate
pout—the one you saved from
childhood, all puff and stomp.
                    Second admit.
Nothing will stop the hand
of god. So learn to run
like a serial killer is behind
you. Hold the scream in
the pocket of your jaw,
the wet sand of it saturated
until the water washes
up through your eye sockets.
                    Third admit.
Betrayal is your most constant
bedfellow. Walk through
it like Athena, each finger of flame

tracing your brain to melt. The slight.
The mishap. The never special.
                    Fourth admit.
You are a terrible, beautiful
force. Flick the granules of
sadness from your lashes
and blink as quickly as possible.
                    Fifth admit.
Every angle is a camera
angle. Flair your nostrils
in abandon. Pretend
bewilderment. Carry the wildness
in your mouth like sacrament.
Grace be. Kneel into it.

Prismatic

What is the sound of one glass breaking? I'm watching the rain. And the shards are spectacular. You should see how they trumpet and dive like beaks into such absent matter. It's not you. It's me. Bring a god of your understanding, because no one else's will do. (this transparent body) Have I told you how I want to write about the way ghosts come through like sheets on wires being pulled across a screen. Each one a year. A sound. A stream. Of consciousness. (bounded) We contain. Not one. But so many versions of this life. Though we never say this life, admitting to something so vast and finally concrete. This living. Come as you are. (in part by two non-parallel) But not really. I said this in theory: famous poets are never ugly. And though we laughed, we were certainly not famous. (plane faces) Though you were beautiful. And, perhaps, theory. Which is neither here nor there. I would go on to keep doing the exact same thing. Transcendental in the giveaway. O how you always (are used to refract or) divide the light.

Gary Smith

Protection from the Rain

Foundation rubbed to the east and
West of my face with just-so strokes.
Eye shadow, bruised as storm clouds,
Over Cleopatra cat eyes.
Cheekbones highlighted—perfect—and

An Anne Francis beauty mark near my
Red pouty lips. Flurries of powder
Conjured from the puff, plus a
Dab of patchouli oil for that
Musky, mother earth, in-heat smell.

And crowning it all, a yellow
Umbrella to keep the rain off
The blond Eva Gabor wig that I
Bought on sale at the Salvation
Army in Aurora, Illinois.

The End of Recess

The mist had turned to rain. On the playground
Cries and shouts, pushing, chasing, running in
Packs, young beasts in a jungle, stalking me
And Annabelle Avery. Trying to
Make me kiss her, the poor kid in class with
Stringy hair and rusty elbows, patched dress and
Worn out shoes, trying to make me kiss her.
I fought to get free, braced my feet in the mud and
Struggled, caught her eyes for a moment—and knew:
She was embarrassed, but wouldn't mind if I
Kissed her, was even hopeful that I would. So
I did, a peck on her wet cheek that she leaned
Forward so tentatively to receive, the
Wet-hair smell of her wafting over me.
Wanting to scrape the back of my hand across
My mouth, but couldn't because she was standing
There in the rain, watching, trusting, letting me
Know she was my responsibility now, as
The bell tolled the end, the end of recess.

The Tempest

Windows are closed, shades drawn.
Rain beats down on the tin roof.
Lightning, one, two—a clash of thunder.
The creek will be over the road by noon.

I shout into the darkness that it's
Time to get up. Holding my breath
Against alcohol that's
Soured the air, I shout louder.
Daddy, get up. Breakfast is ready.

There's a slow movement and then an
Upheaval of bedclothes. The belt
Buckle flashes as he pulls the
trousers up over his nakedness.

Susan Zeni

February Rain: Apache Junction, Arizona

Cactus arms wave in sloshy slant,
stubby V-signs in the rain,
every cell of every porous chamber drenching full, laughing up the
    pour.

Today, no blinders drawn against the heat,
no Harleys kick-assed through the sprawl of motored-homes,
no family names forgotten in the shuffle south,
no desert-caddy leatherettes, blanched heads at the wheel,
no homeboys on home-bound walkers and the next stroke
and the next tumble into the awful rumble of God,
white ambulances hurrying ever near.

Only rain
rain, rain, springing spring,
sweet universe gushing down on all,
arroyos a million fleeting blossoms popping in the parch
of every crack and wrinkle, botox, lift, and aneurystic clot,
mobs of rougeless color, bouquets of endless day.

Richard, Divorced

The brilliant sources of the sun and then Seattle rains,
Jersey boy lured out West in a land fraud scheme,
Vegas cop wanting to marry the call girl in Reno,
you taught me to bleed radiators,
re-light the boiler, string window sash-cords,
toss back Concho del Toro,
mediate Elwood and Frances' nightly scraps,
sniff behind doors for purpling corpses, suicide by Drano, suicide
    by gas,
mop the cellar when the stack backed up,
mousie-tailed tampons twizzled en masse,
the 101 cowboy shooting holes in his wall.

One night you packed your cop boots, brown flannel shirts
and hopped a freight to Twin Falls, Idaho,
to settle a score, your own private Idaho,
waiting between jail and courthouse to gun down the perp
who rape-strangled your daughter in her basement apartment.
"I shoulda taught her better, shoulda taught her more!"

Hours, days, weeks, would I see you again,
my brain stem re-winding the same old scene
from the Western I'd seen as a kid,
little Brandon deWilde, hand on his holster,
shouting, "Shane, come back!"
But you couldn't pull the trigger on him or yourself,
plug him like cardboard on the firing range.

Now in Seattle the rain it rains every day,
as we stand over I-5 on this downtown bridge,
rush hours in our pockets, the Olympics lost in fog,
sighs and semis like solitary parcels drifting
back down rivers of calamity, desire, Lucky Strikes,

flash floods carving arroyos on your impressible skin,
unlike the hooker who never grows old,
popping Cheerios in a Reno motel,
lashed to back of a bottle,
floating farther and farther south
and always saying no.

2022 Poetry Contest Finalists BIOS

Ezra Adamo is a queer trans-guy studying English at Loyola University and is considering a degree in education. He was a runner-up in the 2022 Saints and Sinners Poetry Contest.

Scott Bailey is the author of *Thus Spake Gigolo*. His poems have appeared in Epiphany, Jabberwock Review, Meridian, New York Quarterly, Sand Hills, Subtropics, The Journal, The Ocean State Review, The Southeast Review, and Verse Daily, among others. He received an MFA from New York University and a PhD from Florida State University. Born and raised in Mississippi, he lives in the French Quarter.

Stacey Balkun is the author of *Sweetbitter* and co-editor of *Fiolet & Wing: An Anthology of Domestic Fabulist Poetry*. She is the winner of the 2019 New South Writing Contest as well as Terrain.org's 10th Annual Contest; her work has appeared in Best New Poets 2018, Mississippi Review, The Rumpus, and several other anthologies and journals. Stacey holds an MFA from Fresno State and teaches creative writing online at The Poetry Barn and The Loft.

Danielle Bero was born in Queens to hippie parents who gave her a dose of Shel Silverstein, Tupac, jazz, and classic rock. Bero is a Posse scholar; she has taught in Indonesia on a Fulbright and co-founded a school for students in foster care. She holds a master's in English Education, Educational Leadership, and an MFA from the University of San Francisco. She is a Jack Straw Fellow and Saints and Sinners Festival poetry winner. She has been published in Divine Feminist Anthology, Lavender Review, Quiet Lightning, and Juked, among others. She has a micro-chapbook published by Ghost City Press.

Jeremy Halinen's *What Other Choice* won the 2010 Exquisite Disarray First Book Poetry Contest. His poems have appeared or are forthcoming in Cimarron Review, Court Green, The Greensboro Review, Meridian, Poet Lore, Sentence, and in the anthologies *Best Gay Poetry 2008, Collective Brightness: LGBTIQ Poets on Faith, Religion & Spirituality 2011*, and *Pale Fire: New Writing on the Moon 2019*.

Jamie Kim-Worthington (they/he) is a Korean American transman from Los Angeles, California. They study Latin and Greek and love Anne Carson's writing. Their writing has been published in magazines such as Rice & Spice, Cargoes, and Stonecutters. Other than poetry, they plan to pursue studies in library science, Classical literature and languages, and teaching.

Michael Montlack is the author of two poetry collections, most recently *Daddy*; and editor of the Lambda Finalist essay anthology *My Diva: 65 Gay Men on the Women Who Inspire Them*. His poems have appeared in Prairie Schooner, North American Review, The Offing, The Cincinnati Review, and Poet Lore. His prose has appeared in Huffington Post, Kenyon Review and Advocate.com. In 2020, two of his poems were nominated for Pushcart Prizes and one was a finalist for Best of the Net. He lives in NYC.

Jeffrey Perkins is the author of *Kingdom* which was published by Spork Press in 2020. He earned his MFA from Bennington College where he was the recipient of the Jane Kenyon Memorial Scholarship. His poems have been published in Tupelo Quarterly, The Adroit Journal, Memorious, Rhino, The Cortland Review, and The Massachusetts Review, among others. He was a 2019 Artist-in-Residence at the Watermill Center. He lives in Los Angeles and is currently working on a novel.

Noel Quiñones is a Puerto Rican writer, educator, and community organizer from the Bronx. He has received fellowships from Poets House, the Poetry Foundation, CantoMundo, Tin House, and SAFTA. His work has been published in POETRY, Green Mountains Review, the Latin American Review, Kweli Journal, and elsewhere. He is the founder of Project X, a Bronx-based arts organization; a reviewer of poetry at *Muzzle Magazine*; and an MFA candidate in poetry at the University of Mississippi.

Jen Rouse directs the Center for Teaching and Learning at Cornell College. Her work has appeared in Lavender Review, Sinister Wisdom, SWWIM, Pithead Chapel, The Citron Review, Schuylkill Valley Journal, Mississippi Review, and elsewhere. Her books with Headmistress Press include, *Acid and Tender*, *CAKE*, and *Riding with Anne Sexton*.

Gary Smith has had stories published in James White Review, Amethyst, The Evergreen Chronicles, and Ball State Forum, among others. Two of his stories were finalists for the Saints and Sinners 2020 and 2022 anthologies. He has had plays produced by Mid-America Playwrights Theatre, and one short play given a workshop production by Actors Theatre of Louisville during their Humana Festival. Smith lives with his partner in Springfield, IL.

Susan Zeni has lived in the East Village, Chinatown, Harlem, and Seattle; she now calls Minneapolis home. She won a humanitarian award for a poem in the New York Quarterly and has been published in the Seattle Weekly, Minneapolis Strib, Earth's Daughters, and Landfall, among others. Pre-covid, she organized a monthly dance for women, and got her kicks playing accordion in the all-girl band: *Tsatskelehs*.

SAINTS + SINNERS

2021
NEW POETRY
FROM THE FESTIVAL
poems on the theme of love

edited by
Brad Richard and Paul J. Willis

Judge's Introduction

All of the writers who participated in the Saints & Sinners competition brought a big heart to the work they contributed. As Audre Lorde stated: "Poetry is not a luxury," but that doesn't mean it can't be luxurious! In the winners of the competition, I found the most elegant and luxurious words and ideas that gave voice to the souls of these writers.

Winner Danielle Bero writes: ". . . She is my last thought/watered to flourish like wildflowers in California fields/pushing up through fire/and char/in New York City cement cracks to bloom in colors..." Here, she's speaking not just of the beauty but of the toughness it takes to be beautiful. In her work she captures the ordinary "Sweaters and misplaced cat hair . . ." and the extraordinary "I'm glitter in warm rain . . .," making her audience want to move closer and hear more.

Ezra Adamo displays a phenomenal dexterity with language that opens us up emotionally to his images. "i've never been pretty" begins: "fingers curled, dug, under ribs and/laughing young; i hold rounded/potential for love . . ." He is at the start of a strong career.

Steven Riel, in his poem "I Never Went Back to You," writes with heartbreaking tenderness in recalling an affair from his youth with a man that research shows has passed away. ". . . because I now know you stopped breathing/during the first wave of our plague/ because I would have held you lightly/as you threw up or coughed/ would've stood like a wet boulder at your funeral/whether your kin liked it or not . . ."

Each of these writers creates a shining page in the world of poetry and in the lives of LGBTQ+ writers.

Jewelle Gomez
Judge, 2021 Saints and Sinners Poetry Competition

Editor's Note

Few things are as humbling as reading submissions for a writing competition. Reading through the work of so many talented and imaginative writers is always exciting, both for the astounding discoveries ("how did they *do* that?") and for the sheer range of voices, traditions, identities, urgent declarations, and precise and surprising observations and insights. It's a lot—and it's a joy.

We are thrilled to congratulate this year's winner, Danielle Bero, and our runners-up, Ezra Adamo and Steven Riel, along with our extraordinary finalists. We are deeply grateful to them all for sharing their "shining pages" and to our judge, Jewelle Gomez, for her care in making her selections.

Queer literature is always worth celebrating for the sheer fact that it exists at all. Even in 2021, a middle or high school student somewhere has stumbled upon a poem, essay, comic, or novel that they desperately needed to find—that has saved their life by validating it and giving them permission in turn to use language to convey some sense of their experience and their imagination. We older readers need this work, too, as we continue to grow in our knowledge and appreciation of what it means for ourselves and others to be queer.

That queer literature thrives is due entirely to readers and writers like you. We at the Saints and Sinners Festival, and the Tennessee Williams/New Orleans Literary Festival, are grateful for your support. And we look forward to seeing you when we present next year's festivals, March 22-27, 2022, in the French Quarter of New Orleans.

Brad Richard
Board Member, The Tennessee Williams & New Orleans Literary Festival
Chair, Saints and Sinners Festival Advisory Committee

Danielle Bero

Winner of the 2021 Saints & Sinners Poetry Competition

Cutting Cords with Teeth— another lesbian break-up

My queen
of no kingdom just domain
and patience
food and sleep
baths and arguments

She is the book ends to my library
each book a story in compassion
of truth and innocence, of princesses that save themselves
no white dresses, more like black boots

Sweaters and misplaced cat hair
she pets
and let's be
the feline inside under
human skin
she grooms
and let's free

Mood swings back and forth between our bodies
her rulings
out the bad thoughts
She is my last thought
watered to flourish like wildflowers in California fields
pushing up through fire
and char
in New York City cement cracks to bloom in colors
and reign over the ash and concrete

Skin to skin to skin
to eyes
Clouds as cotton candy as lips
She feels home
to my bones
that have been tossed
and fetched and slobbered
buried and torn
she hugs it out
and I am in.
Again

I pull out each individual tooth
tight rusted pliers   pull hard until pop
release molars cracking
mainly to hear the sound of them tinker in the sink
one by one
clink
and pull back the skin from my mouth
peeling the flesh
kneading it away from bone
like pie dough to the pan
folds and tears sometimes occur
until I am finally
Naked.

I chew on her edges gumming
chipping remaining teeth into powder
We asthma.

And now you are done
of course
and this done feels like the one before
and the one before that
and that .. and that

I get it
I'm difficult
I don't get it
everything is difficult

A different cult of a needy woman
storyline pronounced jaw, strong 9-5
crumbles at midnight
in the safety of floral hugs
now smashed glass slippers
to slice arms
into patterns of lesbian
of mother
of...

I have no words left
She scrubbed them
all away
and left me (sic)

Son of a Butch

I am 34 and 8 together not added
I am a strong believer in poems
        and folded petals of flowers
creased pink aroma
My cabinet will always be stocked w/ Kanye spice
I know every line to them verses with the ad libs
        that speech of modern gospel
a conversation I force with rhythm and punch lines
I'm glitter in warm rain that steams cement
a stomp through mud puddles with fresh J's
        I am the tropics
            the thunder
                the Aries inside your love
Sun and daughter   not quite mother
Rough tender the lion and the lamb
            a kebob of predator and victim
I am woman as a vessel
a design trapped over soul
to Bryson Tiller women of interest

I am 35 and 14 angsty
a strong believer in education with imagination
        rethinking the brick building, paperwork sheets and the
    school lunch trays
my spirit will always be the   NYC skyline
I know every line to The Matrix, we lie is slimy sacs dozing in and
    out
        of protest and complacency
I'm like a sun shower in all its dichotomy bright and chilling in my
    duplicity
I am not American cheese   brick by brick half melting

I am basically 40 years old

I am a strong believer in Jhene Aiko
                    swirling sound bowls from LA epicenters
My spirit will always be the NY city skyline then, now and forever
        to come
under water   inside fire
I know every line to the *Fridays*
                    even on a Monday
I'm like glitter in cement sparkling under fresh J's
I am not afraid of war   I am ready   maybe
les be real, prolly not ready for war but
I put black paint under my eyes
Left Eye to be exact
        bc I am a strong believer in that TLC, Aaliyah and all the
        other fallen black women soldiers
I hold up in my room late at night
                                blunt and posters
my spirit will always be covered
        in rainbow prisms
I know every line to poems written by middle schoolers I Title 1
        forgotten city backstreets
I write their lines inside my palms and sweat them off before it is
        time to recite

I am, I am

Dragging the bottom of my pants from East River
to Lake Toba to Lake Tahoe
I put me over rice
You place me on the rocks
        I am *would you rather..*

73

The Thing is All a Dream That *I Want to Tell You but* *Shouldn't* Because *I Used to Love Her* It Was Once Said

The thing is I am hot pink in my dreams
light apricot when awake
a trick to see how you pronounce it
I want to tell you a story, I shouldn't
it's not clear when the dream ends
and the day starts
so I keep her in the middle all night
I used to love her but her shadow
feels safer than the light bending
her body to find my eyes
hazel in her light from black in the black
it was once said that women are too full
to complete other women
so I break off my ribs for her
to pull apart and make a wish

The thing is she only bit the apple
not to eat it but to see if the act
would switch out man for
curves and emotions turns and devotion
it was all a dream
before any magazines
she flipped rocks and devils advances
instead of glossy pages
she wanted to tell me
a story, she shouldn't
so she used the snake
to carve out my insides
I used to love her
until my cavity became rhythmless
I was beating before
It was once said colors

74

are imagined anyway   .

The thing is I am mostly gray with some purple and blue bruised
    jumping jacks around the eye.
and it was all a dream rainbows represent anything other than
    chasing opaque luck.
of course I want to tell you the story, I shouldn't about the girls and
    the bowl and the fruit and the boring painting of the waxy fruit
    instead of her wetting lips.
I used to love her until her spit turned sour and then bitter from
    rot.
As it was once said I fermented her lips to black her out.

Nefertiti/ititfefeN

I see her on the Montgomery Street corner and untouch her elbow,
    gently
wrinkles smooth out backwards
she unclicks the button and unblocks me
unclicks, follows
                my hand unhits her cheek
red unstings our faces
she puts my pieces back together to then take them apart and again
she unkisses me we unfight over sushi
words unravel from lips backwards into face swallow
unsitting on our shared couch passing the clip back and forth into
    the jar and in an uncut cigar
unhearing Frank Ocean and undirtying the dishes on the coffee
    table
          her lap in Oahu sand unframing our heating bodies
repacking our unpacked boxes and picture frames
unmeeting at a house party in my apartment in Harlem on one two
    fiff on Halloween
              a lion in Timbs and a Ninja Turtle with a snapback
she unfollows me into the bedroom
      unmeet her and men cat call at her to and from the subway
    with dark lips
unpainted nude
without me just ungraduating high school
blood under her fingernails from her last suspension
now unburned and unthrown out by her mom and ex
all her childhood pictures and letters unwritten
in juvey being silent
just before unstealing that cellphone
shivering for a unwave in 30 degree waters
fog skies before starting work at Louis Vuitton
before Jehovah door to door in middle school with mom and dad
before cracking open from jumping on the bed

and cleaning the carpet with a head of stitches
unlearned kissing boys in class
          breasts retreated back into her flesh
all black attire
her uncle untouching her in the same places
she unlearned how to count and read and tie her shoes
she is just a kid with chubby cheeks and noticeable curves
undoing her smile as a toddler
Finally unseeing color pushed through her mother
unborn
unruling the kingdom in her organless crypt of clay pots and cat
     souls.
Pacing for rebirth.

Ezra Adamo
Runner-Up, the 2021 Saints and Sinners Poetry Competition

in his pocket: a figurine of his husband

after rain,
with a small rabbit box,
he walked to the corner

to gather snails
(huddled, strolling)
along the *aspidistra elatior,*

the cast iron plant;
mus(t)(k) of close earth—
lazy-whispers; he is

raw and sober,
and they are
soft; imagined one

behind the ear,
trailed wet to the
eyelid—he blinks

to stand up, close
the box, and take
his mother's hand home.

weathervane

we only know what
          my blood tastes like—

my body never heals
          or dissolves unwanted

parts. gold; i wears a tree
          around my finger and

he wants to bury me,
          he says—starry cheeks

frozen blue. we drink
c   offee, unqualified,

when we feel a lull—
(tepid wind; sweet

rain) and mold
          the dips and hills

of the backs of our
          hands, fingers, to—

gether, barely. i leave
          blood on his soft

foggy skin.

i've never been pretty

fingers curled, dug, under ribs and
laughing young; i hold rounded
potential for love— potential

his veins drape and throb sick;
i wait for new body price,
so i can dip, tangled wet,
beneath lavender and stripped roof

dedicated city whispers: saturday
and sunday aren't times, and
i want to die in france,
baited blush for him or
anyone or—

brick and rail spike—dry-sweet
like i imagine his cologne

Steven Riel

Runner-Up, the 2021 Saints and Sinner Poetry Competition

I Never Went Back to You

i.
Thoroughbred freckles dappled your deltoids
as if you were model & classic statue in one
in the slanted, amber sunbeams
those autumn afternoons.

I marveled at your grown-up realm
where you lined the path to your bed
with stacked newspapers.
Your bathroom's blaring
fluorescence I even embraced
because it spotlit my waking dream
as I'd lather your nape, gape behind your milky back.

Before those weekends,
my undergraduate abdomen had glistened
each solitary Saturday night
in my run-down apartment in the city
where I kicked back damp sheets—
my scrubbed ears a small-town audience
held captive while the upstairs neighbor, a booted clone,
& his first trick of the weekend
pounded hard & bellowed
just above my ceiling,
making my whole being blush.

As a boy, I'd spend Lent studying Jesus' doweled feet,
the tear-drop gash in his side. The body of
Christ stuck to my tongue & stayed stuck—

as if I needed a tutor
before I could savor melting Godiva
in spite of the martyrs.

◆

Your fingertip beguiled me
(I thought I was ugly & undeserving—
I was nineteen) on that velvety sofa
as the theme of your slideshow

drifted towards skin. Mine
pulsed for the sequel. All I ever wanted:
creamy man older man bigger man muscled man,
but what came after easing off your wire glasses
four weekends in a row
wasn't all I wanted after all.

ii.
I never went back to you, till tonight.
An idle Google search turns up a †
after your name. My mind staggers.
Then I track down your death date,
print the black & white yearbook photos
of you at twenty-one, pale & gangly,
in the back row with the Young Republicans,
your tweed jacket & the horn-rimmed glasses
sported by the other prep boys you bedded
(you bragged you bagged scores of them).
That lit-up look on your face I recall,

the kissable up-flip in your upper lip.
—Now I'm on a mission, hunt down
articles you authored, a color shot
of the modest memorial your rich
but restrained parents donated
to your alma mater, their online obituaries
lengthy because they were prominent
yacht- & golf-club Pilgrim-descended industrialists,
& so were you, their tersely mentioned,
previously deceased eldest scion,
the IIIrd, who spilled his seed. On me.

◆

It wasn't *Love Story*.
You kept miles away from "Love
means never having to say…,"
from introducing me to the mansion,
where even if I'd possessed a Main Line pedigree,
top-drawer manners, twill from J. Press,
& never, ever alluded to sunny afternoons,
by contrast Jenny Cavalleri's fiery red dress
would have seemed a flair fit to be married.

iii. Mayflower Cemetery

because your brother didn't answer my letter

because I figured that like my brother
an unmarried & childless son
you'd be buried beside your parents

because at first I didn't see
your cutting-board-sized stone

because it was that day each October
when a whole generation of leaves lets go

because I now know you stopped breathing
during the first wave of our plague

because I would have held you lightly
as you threw up or coughed

would've stood like a wet boulder at your funeral
whether your kin liked it or not

because to rip back dandelions & crabgrass
& scrape with my nails broken pine needles
filling in the letters of your name,

I will kneel six feet from you
year after year.

A Cage's Lament

Yes, Mr. Pigglesworth, you wipe your beak
against my kiln-baked skin, but I
want to hold you—really hold you.
You know me as The Obstacle,
without understanding
that inside I become lava
whenever your feathers brush my bars.

If only I could chirrup and inform you
your incessant sawing and clawing
get you nowhere—
that I'm welded wrought iron
with recessed rivets and no exposed nuts.

It's not in my power to fall apart.
I can only hold up
your coop cup, cuttlebone,
jungle gym, and full-length mirror
so that together we can admire
the long tail of your red tuxedo. Oh.

But that strumpet Mrs. Smith
uses me to woo and ensnare you.
While she coyly calls you
Mr. Neurotic, I'm the slave hoisting her gifts
day and night: the tropical fruits, the soft-wood
toys you gnaw. If I could produce
snapshots of the former Misters she's hand-reared,
you'd cease to crave her stroking.

Even if I found a way to froth up
into gossamer netting and become an aviary,
I couldn't compete with her bottomless wallet.

While you slumbered, snug
inside my fitted night-cover,
she told her plaid nephew
she's provided for you, her final companion,
in her will. As for me,
if I'm lucky, I'm destined for a yard sale.

At least I'm always on hand to hear you
mimic the clock.
          If only I could evaporate.
At least, my pet, you take it all out on me,
instead of plucking yourself.
          If only I could rust away.
At least I winced for you
during your youthful, panicked attempts
to bite through me.
          If only I could unlatch.
At least I witness those attacks,
though they've become habit,
become halfhearted.
          If only I could speak.

Today, Brother, You Would Have Turned 56

We *did* become cheerleaders in the end.

After high school games against Northfield,
secretly we'd stomp, clap, & pretend
we wore their squad's sado-genteel
red leather gloves. How hickster uncool!—
we'd mimic them—*slap sla-sla-sla slap*—
idolizing instead our fluffy-sweater school's
troupe, who flounced when the right rim ball dropped with a tap.

College. In this snapshot, you lifted one boulevard-wide banner's
      side,
shirt tied high to flaunt Coppertoned skin. Your thin gray shorts
suggested the rest. How pretty undergraduates paraded in Pride.
Head-cheerleader politico queer, I led the *hey-hey, ho-ho* retort.

No other person on Earth mocked those red leather gloves.
My thumbs drum our chant beside this photo I love.

Ken Anderson

Photo

Where have the steps led if not your door?

(An apartment like a small life
like all the other small lives
paper-thin wall to wall.)

You welcomed me,
I stepped inside, and now
we've printed copies of the day.

Only you could decipher the birthmark,
the eye, the nod. Only you could see
what wasn't there, the ghost
the camera couldn't catch, the developing best
of me, yes, working my way out of words
I turned on myself like a gun,
out of a crumpled paper bag as big
as the night, out of the lost perspectives
like a Hall of Mirrors…out of me,
in short, into you, into the bedroom
and all the other rooms of you.

We have traveled a long way to strip
by the bed, to bare our muscles, freckles, scars.
You read, by touch, my body's sensitive Braille.
Blind, deaf, and mute, we talk.

And now you have gone deeper
into me than anyone else, into my poems, my past,

my promises, inside the house,
behind the locked door, the lowered shade.

I didn't know I could let you in me this far,
didn't know I could face you or turn away, could fuck
with a dancer's grace, grab you with my body, see
what I could do or just lie back and, bent
beneath you, see what you could do, or just lie back
and, legs around you, see what we could do
to reach such perfect ecstasy.

Perhaps

Perhaps the phone stopped ringing just
before you picked it up. I think you'd lie
on the couch, let your life pass, and never give a damn.
We missed our chance, a near miss, but we missed,
ahead, yet second to the luck of things. The letter
with the wrong address, the phrase
that almost says how you feel, the subtle plea
in your gaze, all this, all little things destroy.
The great advantage lies with those
who reach the phone in time, who make a move,
who catch the conversation underneath the words.
"How are you? Call me. Hear?" I shook
to hear your voice today accepting everything
just like that theme in Mahler's Tenth, the saddest *yes*
that music ever said. Perhaps someday we'll walk
beside each other down a street and never notice
who we are or could have been. Perhaps someday
I'll find another in the crowd, but I'll remember
how we missed our chance, the two of us
alone, beside each other on the couch, divided
by ourselves.

One Hour More

In tune, but
out of time and luck, we can't catch up or wait
till stars fall
into place. For life's no Capra film
where lovers can keep up and kiss. Ill -starred,
like Shakespeare's two, we're close,
but, for the wall between, too far. I've tried
to think
of what to do or say, but then
how can we shoot our scene
of love
at first sight
once again? Later, when we met and talked,
then dined and toured the bars,
I knew the formulaic plot,
the hokey grade B movie end. The villain turns
into a hero, but too late—a trick
to win our sympathies. Sometimes
I string our days and nights together
like the notes
of a slow romantic melody, how we agreed
in voice and gesture, other ways
in bed
and played each other there
at just the perfect pitch. At times, I wish
that we were more a new piano piece,
an atonality, no major or minor chords. But then
I'd rather one brief song, one hour more
with you, the hour
that we missed back then
when we stepped
out of time.

You Knew

You knew—one glance—how I would be
with you and now have been and will.
You taught me how to make up time,
and I held nothing back, sweet Chris.
Lover, friend, please write it down
for me and everyone
that I held nothing back, no kiss, not one.
I flashed a flashlight into the dark
labyrinthine basement of my heart.

I carry you within, without.
I carry you, yes, everywhere—
a photographic negative
through all the busy terminals,
through all the midnight city streets
to every narrow random room
where I lie down with someone not the same,
with less than could have been—and was.

Among the laughter in the bar
I hear you say my name again,
and when I dance, I dance with you.
No one can touch me now unless
he touches me the way you do.
Your heartbeat keeps the beat with mine
if he does things you used to do,
but only if his body's yours.
No one can kiss and taste like you.
To me, you love me in his place.

And when I'm walking home at night,
I feel a wolf is stalking me
or waiting patiently by the door.

Only then, will your lonesome ghost—a ghost
that haunts me through the hours—
turn his moonlit ice-blue eyes away.

I blow out the candle by the bed
and draw your eager dream to me.
I draw you to me closer still.
You roll on top. You tongue my mouth.
You push my knees against my chest.

Some lovers say goodbye and leave.
I never left. I never will
though I will never see you, Chris, again.

Steven Cordova

The Love Poem

has always said more about the poet
than it has the beloved.

The beloved's easily replaced;
the poet's the essential thing.

It's the difference, perhaps, between
praising & being praised.

To praise artfully requires talent;
to be praised prettily, patience.

These days there's more & more poets
who find themselves more easily replaced.

It's a beloved's market
but patience has gone out of style.

Still the love poem, sturdy thing, lives on.
It stars the poet; co-stars the beloved.

Slapping the Ghost of a Ghost-Love

for the Phantom, once more

I slap you for leaving.

Leaving, you are, always, already, coming back.

That, too, is why I slap you.

I slap you for the coming-back that is always, sooner or later, to come.

I hate you leaving as much as I hate you coming back and more, much more than I hate you going (going, gone) ....

I slap you—slap you, slap you, slap you—on the left side of your face for the leaving. I slap you—slap you, slapped you, slap you—on the right side for the coming back—and for the not.

At 54

I'm six away from sixty,
not sure why numbers transfix me,

why I let myself get misty
over heartbreaks, ancient histories:

Once you dared to kiss me
smack dab in the middle of the city:

We were ten away from fifty,
high & a little tipsy.

Everyone said, "Oh, what a pity"
once our love turned bitchy

The good, the bad—it happened, quickly.
That's why numbers transfix me.

Dante Fuoco

Yesterday

Yesterday I made
you a sandwich
I thought by then
you'd kiss me the onions—how
did you find the
onions I pickled
with vinegar
I couldn't afford
and the bread was
from a woman
who spoke to me
in French
and I don't even
eat meat but
there I was arranging
a cured thing
for you.
How banal
how tired
I know
winning a man
over with food
though it changes
when a man gives
a man the sandwich?
and
I am not a man
not
when I made you

97

the sandwich
I was a parcel
a package I was
sent being sent
and, oh
someone who
I never cared for
wrapped me
jostled me in line
and threw me
on the counter
the whole transaction
was far too long
they're always
too long
the man sending me
the man processing me
were separated with
bulletproof glass
doors with brass handles
that you'd tug
toward the ceiling
and one man opening
his door meant the
other couldn't open
his and in between
was a stuffy space
was where
I had to wait
for the two of them
to make up their minds
on how I'd ever reach you.

sheet shopping

he and I are hard
to touch
at night.

i shepherd hope
when he sleeps.

he'll spit
in his hand
in the morning

this old
spice man

he takes me

                    sheet shopping

in my dream

                    tumble dry low

he gives me time

                    thread counts

he gives me his hand

how soft, how soft

                    how soft

it is
this comfort

                    he can buy

what is there to hope for on a highway when all highways are dead

This dried-out river of going has got
me nauseous, and what is there to hope for
on a highway when all highways are dead.

I've just flown "home." We rush home
on I-376 for a football game that's
already started. Against the radio

I press: "Can't we talk?" My father explains
"it's a very important game," to which my
mother adds: "The Steelers have to win."

Can't we talk? I should say to the trees
that border our drive—should say
by way of begging, a plea to the dead

silent things, whose limbs have shriveled
into roots, craggly and black—who
by standing sentry to our rush

are huffing human exhaust. What the fuck
they are saying, my parents and the trees
each stuck in their own way. The outrage

of loss has got all of us reaching. What the fuck
are they doing: Those boys, those men
cleating green in the winter. I don't care

for their trampling, though I, too,
am a man, hawking my path.
And here I am, late. I've missed the fall.

I've missed color. Pittsburgh. My stomach
is a spool the valleys tug. I close my eyes.
Once this highway didn't exist. The valleys

that sicken me are ancient of course.
I see again the trees, the so many trees
and—there: a slaughtered brown body

at the highway's lip. This valley. This girly
valley—she has something to say, having
been made to kiss the asphalt that mans

her curves, having done it for so long.
And it's not quite listening, how the road
bends in concession. And—I was wrong:

it's not quite death what the trees are reeking.
So today what is it but enduring? The trees,
those bare bodies—they're fending off death

this winter. To keep from dying they must
shed their leaves. They know energy.
They know what it means to conserve to take

to wait to wait. They can wait for what it is
they need. When the Steelers score
a touchdown my parents cheer. Can't we talk?

I could say again, though this time I tend to it
like a prayer: alone. Can't we talk? I ask myself
until the tree of me arches to some great granite light.

Stephanie Glazier

Poet's Prayer

Let me struggle and desire.
Let me run toward joy

as the girl to the lake.

These hills were steeper when I was younger.
I remember sleeping and my body straining
against the upholstery of our car at night.
Blues, from the radio.

And the day my mother stopped the car
at a crest
with a chisel
and her children
complaining.

She scored a declaration for her man
and signed the remnant of a tree.
I watched her put her name into something
once living.

Just now it's the last of summer
the wind pitches plenty
and light blesses the water.
The sky is surreal   it does not stop.

Call me young.
Call me not disappointed enough in love.

Standing At the Door I Was Born Behind

That the apartments were still there, I could not believe,
that they stood across from a Seven-Eleven made me believe.
The number five at my front, my birth certificate at the ready—
for what? I couldn't bring my other hand up.
The terrible green color, must have been the twenty fourth coat and
    the cheap
gilt handle of the knocker, the knob. I couldn't bare it.
Whomever was inside and I could hear that someone
was, it wasn't my mother.

T.S. Leonard

Love Song

The man I love will be a mother
fucking monster, a milky sea with a heart
the size of a whale. A whole season of a person;
he'll change. He will be my sister

in the sense that our love makes him
cry easily. Like us across the Badlands watching
clouds break, the man I love will be a storm:
he'll form, he'll fury, and I will remain

a prairie.

River Phoenix

Your favorite actor died today, too young, but so are you,
rightfully tantruming against pricks, pins and needles,
every string you can pull, the fibrous final tethers
keeping you in this ungodly room with me
here forever the first of November in 1993—

But later I will imagine what could come next:
if you were to rip free from your failing machinery
and rise up in your gown, now glowing, floating,
only for your hot feet to hit the linoleum, running,
you say, *let's get the hell out of here*, and we're off—

flashing by untouched dinner trays and yesterday's paper
ghosts (I've never seen you so fast!), already dated cork-
board, past the dying and the just-born, bounding whole
wards (I'm trying to keep up), flying through the waiting
room to tumble after you and out the sliding doors—

memory jog over our pillaged blocks and we run
this town where we came up dancing—we are now
the most alive living boys this city has ever seen!—
you, redding, trailing wires, Ginger-graceful in evading the
fallen bluebirds scattered on the quiet concrete; and we

still make it to the water's edge with all our old haunts we
rushed past behind us, your sudden wings whisk the ram-
part and we stop, on heel; you, panting, looking finally
at the long blue, and glancing back for a split-second,
half-grin; but even in this version, I can't catch you.

She shuts your eyes and I walk home alone
to our stoop, the candy bowl with your sign—*take*
as many as you want—emptied, and it's the same

one I use to carry you the day to that very river
when we let you go, and just then, the wind picks up—

common rush

once again i have confused love for owning

a home; or those feelings of desire for what

i myself still lack. but it can be arranged,

like tatami mats it can be pushed aside

in favor of some more western style.

yet love is many-sided and endures

the changing taste of any nation.

boymom

We had a daughter and we named her
hopeless, so she had something easy to
rebel against, a wish that wasn't pink
or a ribbon; hopeless is a grown man
who changed his name, too, to
tender, so he has something hard to
reach toward, a strength that isn't rage
or an engine; tender is a son now who
we never had to name ourselves—
family, so we had learned to call it, to
fight for, a sentence that can't be finished
or a bow; we had a curve now and
we named it after us. We are hopeless,
tender family and we have ourselves
to choose and to name and to be-
long

Helena Lipstadt

Derring-Do

Alright, there was nothing medieval about it.
Except the flash of steel, the snap of your cape
when you swung off your Honda 250.

The weight of that bike, like a steer
with handlebars and I, no weakling,
could barely hold on.

or was it you, slip sliding, or was it me,
in the flip of an eye, losing into the pitch black
of your hair, so dark it had no beginning.

All I wanted, all I wanted, was to tangle
with you, between you, between you,
the bike and your butch girlfriend.

New Content

The grass is sunwarm and green.
It is spring in Krasnogruda.
I am lying on a bed of earthworms.
I don't hear them, I don't smell them,

I don't care that they're working
their horizontal way
to the big red door
of the Manor House.

Milosz's ghost lingers in the eaves.
I didn't come here to meet
a Serbian blonde.
I came to unbury

Poles, preferably
from Warsaw,
preferably long lost.
But Ksenija teaches me to say,

"Hello my friend"
in Polish, then
in Serbian, for luck.
She leads me

from the library
to the dock.
She lays her hand
on my shoulder

names six kinds
of shorebirds
that nest

on Holny Lake

pulls back
the reeds
nods to where
the otters slip
into the water.

Names Go Traveling with No Valises

My mother's names:
Bala Basia Bayla Barbara

My father called her *Bala?*
every day around the house,
with a lift at the end
where are you, my love?
as if afraid he lost her,
which is how I know her,
two soft syllables, sometimes made softer,
Basia, and I melt,
a child in love with her mother,
and also afraid
she would lose her.
In disguise, her false identity
card stamped "Barbara,"
strangely English and foreign, but there
in black and white is her young face.

My father's names:
David Dovid'l Tadzik Tadeus

She called him *Tadzik,*
without fear, until the end
when everything splintered
and she searched for him desperate
if he stepped out of sight.
But in Yiddish he was Dovid'l,
a young man again and beloved,
he had a harp to play.

These are the names of his parents:
Hentsche and Hirschel from Warszawa

These are the names of her parents:
Adele and Aron Ber from Sieradz

They board the train,
they disembark,
they start over.

All by myself,

I am having an affair
with you

you don't care
you don't know
ty lubie

I'm wrapping
my lips
around you

your tongue
your throat
your body of cherries

your smell, familiar
as an orchard
of dangling fruit, fallen,

then folded in a cone of paper
I don't want to be rid
of you, I can't

it would be like
tearing the pink belly from my peonies,
the bark off my tree

Freesia McKee

Hummingbird Vows

late September
Milwaukee forgot
first hummingbird

Home again after a year away. Blueberries and yogurt. No piano. My mom says it lives in the gym now at Rufus King High School. Here is where I can be myself with precedent, no nothing in front. My mom and dad at the gate. Don't recognize me with this new hair. I don't care. My mother is committed to consistency. My father drove. In the middle of the night, my partner comes home to my home, closing the door and I am waiting for her in my sister's old room, a darker, greener room. Trying to be quiet. A photograph of plums on the wall. A picture of a white fence and winding vine. In forward fold, something in my back released that had been stuck for years. Or at least a year. Because I'm back. Even standing feels different.

black-eyed susans
efore we met
his marsh covered with fill

My dad says that yesterday, he set a red towel outside to dry. It attracted hummingbirds because, he says, anything that color beckons them. Blood, fire hydrants, the startling eyes of white bunnies. Crab apples, chokecherries, tulips, stop signs. A red coffee cup. A red bicycle. Hummingbirds have no use for most of these items; an acute need for some. Like us. My mother says she is downsizing. She asks us if she can get rid of some stuff. Science fair poster boards. Stuffed animals. Her wedding dress from marrying our dad.

fox tail cattail
squirrel tail
lily pad rudder

I've come home to marry my friends. To perform the marriage, to officiate. But because a marriage is a public event, and because I've arrived in Milwaukee without an appropriate outfit, my dad drives me to a thrift store where I find a cotton, knee-length red dress. "The classic wrap dress!" my mother affirms when I bring it home. But it isn't quite right. Instead, I will wear a black outfit. Black to a wedding: Is it bad luck? In this country, most clergy wear black. I'm not clergy, per se. I will wear a long white jacket from my mother's closet over the black.

window is a pond
marriage is a window
we say look for foxes

If my friends and I were Catholic (or still Catholic), I wouldn't be able to do this with them. Because I am a woman. Because I am gay. In front of a century of people, my friends make partnership happen their own way. After the wedding, my mother says that she remembered, mid-ceremony, the she also wore that white jacket when she married her wife in the kitchen two years ago, just five of us there. My mom's marriage to my stepmother is an auspicious occasion to connect to today.

even the leaves
are subject
to change

Days later, when I return home, another home, where I live, I dream about foxes, a whole family at the marsh where we walked the day after we arrived. In the dream, I am faced with my ex-girlfriend who has brought her new lover to my house. The new girlfriend is wearing a red scarf like in a photo I saw accidentally online on another friend's page the day after I perform wedding. When I wake up, I try to forget the dream by reading a book called Family Resemblance. It's not just about how you look, what you wear. There was a point at which I needed to move to another city to establish a queerness independent of my family's. "You're Pat's daughter?" "You're whose partner?" It got awkward. Almost no one could understand it. Because, our culture believes, gay people are supposed to exist alone, one to a family.

red-centered
white hawthorn blossoms
petal the road

On her honeymoon, my friend experiences the kind of shame that is so embarrassing it must be shared. So she texts me: she's accidentally spilled a stranger's cremains. In a bookstore in Kansas City, reaching across the desk to shake the bookstore owner's hand, she accidentally knocked over what was left of Victor. "Please say a prayer for him or something," she says, distraught. "The owner is trying to clean the floor." Fourteen-hundred miles away, I light a candle. "Victor was a poet!" she writes. The situation is so terrible and human that it makes me laugh out loud, alone in my kitchen. I decide not to tell her, yet, that this will be a perfect honeymoon story.

Out of the Tank

I like thinking about the animals
who spend their whole lives in the ocean,
tending to each other, satisfying their affairs in a single
atmosphere. I like thinking about how air joins
with itself like water does, and the in-between
place where the two spheres connect. It gives me solace
when I remember we never really get rid of anything.

Don't shit where you eat,
my ex-girlfriend used to lament
about friends who dated delinquently.
It always seemed like such a crude dictation
of another's new buoyancy. Neither of us knew
that I would leave her, then, moving
the year after with a jet-skiied love to Miami
where sunbathers scar the beach
and manatees move like ghosts.

I see human swimmers having sex in the water
every time I visit the state park here. It's easy to tell
when someone isn't playing a game.
There were three couples today, now four
on this beach, who hooked up with each other
like touching islands of seaweed. I sit with the faces
of my feet firm in the sand, hiding behind a book, watching
the woman I've chosen snorkel and look for new fish.

*This morning at home, the dog whined for so long
because he knew we were there, floating in salt.*

In the water, my partner snorkels alone, her lower back poised
over the soft dip. I watch her wet nape tip towards the clouds
as I would watch anyone I love

investigate, she'll later reveal, a burrowing
fish who sits at the mouth of her den,
daring an extension of bait.

Mirage Equality

On the internet, someone asks,
Does your country allow SAME
SEX MIRAGE?

> Another person responds. *It is a little*
> *like a mirage, isn't it?*

In this online forum, forbidden by mods
and admins from "discussing politics,"
yet joined by our "political" relationships (it's a queer group

> after all), it's hard to say
> what's real.

Someone else in the group polls,
If you were in charge
of a small country, what

> *would be your first law?*
> "Equality" seems to be the most popular,

followed closely by "clothing-optional."
I wonder. What does equality look like
stripped down? Equality is more than same-sex

> marriage, a mirage.
> *Never give up hope*, another poster declares.

I found the love of my life after 29 years
of searching and I've never looked back.
First comes love, then comes mirage.

> *If we're still together in a couple of years*, my friend

tells me she's said to her new boyfriend, *I'll want to marry you.*

I visit my hometown after a few months away.
I learn that two of my friends are getting a divorce.
The roommates who've lived together most of my life

are parting ways. Heartache is real. The lives of people around me
change quickly, which means my life could change quickly, too.

On the return to my girlfriend,
I pick up
my phone in the airport and scroll through news

I've already seen. I leave the conversation over and over,
turning firm in my hands a bright silent mirage.

I am away for some days,
but expect our lives to be the same
when I return. Are our stable apartment,

pets, car, a mirage? I'm hungry for a broader vocabulary
of intimacy, a serious description, but all I can find is
mirage.

I feel want in my throat. As an artist,
my goals can hit offbeat. Once, dozens of people brought
me their questions while I sat quiet as a promise. I attempted answers

for almost everyone. *Will love ever not hurt?* one woman
asked.
*How could I be so unlucky? How could I
be so lucky? Something's gotta give, right?*

121

What We Saw

Anja and I started walking at the beach. We walked among the tourists in the neighborhoods. We walked past the religious and the irreverent. We walked past the tattooed and the straight. We walked in close proximity to poverty and hyper-wealth. We walked past a man pushing a BBQ grill. We walked until we were hungry for dinner. We walked past Chloe's house. We walked past a lesbian couple holding hands with matching hairdo's and I wasn't sure if I should make eye contact with my own kind. We walked and we talked about language. We walked past the North Beach Bandshell and a green blazered man wearing a comical top hat and a live band setting up and young married swing dancers getting ready to move and we stopped and we watched for a while. I pointed to the sound technician and told Anja he was the kind of guy I used to date in college. We walked past restaurants flying the rainbow flag, their waiters carrying hamburgers on square plates. We walked past what Anja said must be the fashion district of South Beach. We walked past a woman tucking an enormous breast back into her dress after feeding her baby. We walked past a middle- aged man wearing a trench coat adorned with dozens of amulets. Anja and I walked past a bookstore and we walked in and almost nobody was in there. We walked past walls covered in shiny CDs. We walked past drug stores and tourist shops sporting shirts emblazoned with words like *USA* and *Bitch*. We walked past strollers. We walked past tables of unhappy and happy couples and couples in-between. We walked down streets that will sink someday. We walked North and we walked West. We never got tired, but Anja's shoes caused blisters. We walked until darkness fell and we were not scared. We walked into someone who told us we must have had a good day at the beach. We walked until Anja told me I've changed. We walked and had a long discussion about Medusa. We walked until we needed to refill our water bottles. We walked and repeated the process. We walked with cameras in our pockets. We walked past pairs of people we didn't know were couples. We walked past couples who didn't know they would become couples.

We walked until we saw a billboard for concrete manufacturers. We walked until Anja took a photo of a medium-sized lizard, and then we walked and we looked for more lizards. We walked until I texted Jade. We walked and we talked about marriage. I told the Anja wrong information and I walked us in the wrong direction. We walked until we needed to charge our phones. Anja and I walked so far that I don't remember some of it. We stopped to use the bathroom. I saw platters of pastries, free samples, but they were not for us. When we started walking, we didn't know when we'd stop. Anja ate gelato and I drank coffee and we both felt satisfied. We talked about and interpreted dreams as we walked. We kept our shoes on the whole time as we walked. We walked behind an old man holding hands with a younger woman in a minidress. I wasn't sure if I was a tourist or not. We walked until the end of the road, and then we turned left and then right. We talked about stopping to write poems on our walk. We talked about mothers after we saw one. We saw a car covered in large lipstick decals like a giant had kissed it. We walked and we saw a cat. We walked to the Jewish Museum. We tried to walk inside, but they were closed. We walked past many stores with windows full of items we were uninterested in purchasing. We walked past a movie set, the cameras rolling. We walked past one of those shitty pop art galleries where they sell bright-eyed paintings of stylized dogs and Marilyn Monroe. We walked past more of them. We walked and we talked about what we were up for. We walked and we talked about PhD programs, about sellouts, about various corners and the art world. We talked about monthlong festivals. We walked and told stories to each other and we found ourselves hilarious. We walked and discussed sushi. We walked and were bougie. We walked and we talked about how we loved walking. All this, while walking. We walked and there were things to see everywhere we looked. We walked and it smelled like sewage. We walked and we talked about thongs and underwear. We talked about alcoholism and spaghetti strap dresses. We talked about 8th grade. We talked about jobs. We talked about shyness. We talked about how to address untenable fears. We talked about swimming. We talked about our friends and we talked about their breakups. Anja received a text and we talked

123

about that. We talked about plants. We talked about our plans for tomorrow. We talked about pronouns. We walked to the library and we walked upstairs. We looked at books and we laughed at them. Then, we talked about history. We talked about the difference between trolleys and busses. Then we took the bus. Then we walked more. Then we drove home.

Charlotte O'Brien

The day after Kamala Harris debates Mike Pence

I take to my bed at 3pm
like some Victorian lady, overcome
by fatigue, cloaking my shoulders;
crawling parasitic across my thighs
seeping down the length of my spine.

It could be any number of maladies—
stress, menses, menopause. The acrid
taste in my mouth
which could be a sign
of terminal or mental illness, or just
disappointment, hard, hard worn.
My aching heart
the same
as all the aching hearts
right now, like my child upstairs
who tells her computer
"I am lonely."

A slow, slow incremental
dying. A sputtering light inside
my body
petering out.
I will close my eyes
to all of it
for now.
But at 3am my heart,
flung across the room
from inside a deep sleep,

will wake me like a sudden plunge
into the coldest water, wanting to know

Where am I?
What the hell is going on?

Translocation (What it comes down to)

1.
Over drinks
in a San Francisco bar
she looks at you, her eyes hard
blue. *One day*, she says,
you'll leave me.
It's possible
you are too old
to be cavorting all day
in bars and book stores.
Your twenty-year-old self had imagined,
by now you'd own a house—
the kind that is clean
and poured with sunlight, children
streaming in and out.
You've begun to understand
you don't want this exactly.

2.
You go shopping for sex toys
in the Castro. You want
to hold her hand,
and kiss her in public
forgetting
something as simple
as a kiss, could be locked and loaded.
You've begun to understand
you are now a target. She is wary
in airports. She pulls away
without warning. *They would kill me
first, and then rape you*, she says.
In your bones, you know this is true.
You've begun to understand

this is not the same
as kissing a husband.

3.
In the night, she wakes you—
her cough, the hoarse hack
of a smoker, and you know then,
she's sick. Her body burning
beside you, sweat pearls on her forehead.
The fierceness of love
is your bottom line. You have cradled
her body with yours, clutching
her muscles, her bones opening
to you: ilium, ischium, pubis.
You have fingered
the hollow of her clavicle; traced
the blades of her scapula; parted
her tendons. You have licked her wounds.
Even the cat, who has slept between you
all night, climbs aboard her chest
to peer at her face.

4.
In the morning, you bring her tea,
but she wants whiskey.
You forage for your clothes.
I'm sorry, she says.
I know it all comes down to sex.
And this is a joke, because you've told her,
you're only there to fuck. *I love
your body*, she tells you,
I love that bra. She studies
the way you lift your breasts
into its black lace. She watches you
snap yourself back into place.
She says: *I want to show your body*

how in love with it I am.
You hand her the full weight
of your right breast.
For next time, you say.

5.
It comes down to the details:
The way she slices
an onion, with her fingertips
clenched as she cuts; the way
her hair falls across one eye—
a mess of curls; how she leans
back into the tub, her eyes closing
to the sound of your voice
reading poetry; her body,
incandescent in the watery half-light;
how the cat folds his paws
beneath him and listens too.
You realize, it's these
small moments
that are saving you.

6.
At the door, she sucks on her cigarette.
You read the pause in her exhale.
I've realized, she says,
why I'm angry. You nod,
because you understand
the unattended child
learns to rock herself to sleep
watching ghosts
from her bed, she learns
to tamp down her fear
and now you are leaving
to return to your children
who clamor at your gate.

Dislocated by loss, their home
is your body. Body of love;
body of sex; body of grief;
body of giving
birth to their bodies.
You offer yourself up,
and in turn they are yours.
You've begun to understand
that you have offered yourself
to her, in all these ways
without knowing
if it is enough.

Jessica Sampley

Elvis Bearing Witness

*—after hanging a portrait of Elvis (painted by my momma in 1980)
in our new house*

He was a good boy.
His life-sized oil portrait guarded our hallway.
Oh, he loved his momma—
as if loving his momma was his ticket to heaven.

His life-size oil portrait guarded our hallway,
bore witness to calloused fingers that clutched and bruised tender
     biceps.
Still, Momma thought she was Daddy's sole ticket to heaven,
so she stayed, not too much harm was done.

Why acknowledge calloused fingers? Let them touch and bruise.
     Tender biceps
grow stronger and learn to suppress, anyway.
So Momma let him stick around; not too much harm was done.
We all knew she always loved him more than us.

Grow stronger. Learn to suppress, anyway.
We like to think he loved his momma.
Momma always knew she loved him more than us.
Wasn't he such a good boy?

Spanish Moss

Bon Secour, Alabama
For my momma

Prelude:

Spanish moss drips
from live oaks,

hangs from limbs
that dive

towards the earth.
It survives,

despite summertime droughts,
a week or two of winter.

Brittle and despondent,
it hangs like

unconditioned hair,
split ends

trying to capture
every last drop

until there's nothing left,
and it falls

like ash
to the ground.

Epilogue:

We saw it hanging everywhere
that day in Bon Secour, when we parked
outside the gates of the Swift-Coles house.
We walked in. I found a piece on the ground.
It crunched in my hand, already dead.
Mosquitoes swarmed, and I swatted
while her eyes glazed over, watched
the sun set over the old nets on that washed-up
shrimping boat, leftover to rot after Frederic.

Two weeks later, when my sister called
to give me the bad news, I was bucket-perched,
pitching short toss to my ball players.
colonoscopy tumors malignant
My grip on those raised laces loosened
then tightened then loosened again.
Red dirt pools clotted at my feet.

That night, I dreamt I found her choking
on a mouthful of Spanish moss, briny water
seeping from the corners of her mouth.
When I ran to her, her jaw clenched tightly
around the gravity of 72 years of loss.
Obstinance and insolence got you here.
You could have prevented this.

And like so many times before, she walked out
into the tannin water, though she's never learned
to swim, a mouthful of bitterness strangling her.
This time, I'm afraid it may do her in.
I woke up screaming *just open your mouth*
open your mouth open your mouth.
I'll take it from you.

Samantha Tetangco

Thirteen Ways of Staring Through the Flames

The world   was on fire

and we   dropped   off
   one by one—

   ashes   to   ashes

                        & dust unto
   dust,

                              until we are
   all listening

                      to Otis Redding

and Al Green,   trying

   to mend   what has been
broken

or reach   with tired arms
           through   the smoking trees
                   and scrub jay's song

                        with zero
           promises
      of rain.

   Why are we surprised?

We left the fields

untended,

    let the wellsrun dry.

            And we   all wonder

       how   the promised land
became

                                  the
hell
      we've created.

And we   all wonder

how   we keep
  driving through,   down

one stretch
      up another

        until
        we are   flames

          licking country
          side,
             black fog
          like death   moving in.

We cast the   matches

  into the fire,   after all.

When flame touched

fast flame,

                      there was   no beginning,

                          no end, before nor after,

                              only
                              fire on fire

while we   bore
             witness

        waiting by open doorways.

    The hills
        turned to ash.

               There,
                   in the center,

                  we held
                               our tongues
                        against roofs

                       until the fire
passed.

             Our cars became husks.

        Silent houses turned
                  to bones

             somehow still standing.

Married Couple, circa 2008

We used to live inside a shoebox.   Do
                youremember   how
you used to wake early
how you'd light the stovetop   before the
sunrose,   and the blue flame   would
danceover your tired face   how every
day   I took a
broom to the floors.   Your
dog hated the sound   of
sweeping, ofour feet   brushing too
fast   on tiles, of
you and I   falling   into
bed.
        I'd climb the fence to the roof
so I could breathe,   once climbed   beneath
your desk, and I should have known
how I would make my palms   a
heavybowl and attempt   to wash us clean.
But
you never told me   you were a well
andbefore long   my arms grew heavy and we
both forgot I needed those hands   for
myself.

Married Couple, Early Morning, circa 2016

In the morning, she

                wake

s humming. She sets our
kettle

on the stove to   boil.
Today, she'll make
           candles

    and gluten-free   bread.
    She'll want to   walk the dogs.

        She'll come into   my
        room as I write at my   desk

    carrying   fresh-cut roses,
    her kiss,   an absent-minded

            reminder that
      here we are,

            once again,
    in the middle of   things—

            I'll shut my eyes

      and pre-   tend
           this   is every morning.

And then I'll   open them.

138

Marriage, Triptych

She lays with her hand on his bare back, her arm outstretched as if reaching for more than his paper skin. Seeing them there, in the bed, which has been their bed long enough for the mattress to hold their shape, tells us something of the delicate gift of human touch.

After the fall, your grandmother, fifteen years a widow, tells us how the nurse scrubbed her back with a coarse sponge. *Oh*, she said, her eyes closed in remembering, *it felt so good*, and it's hard not to think of the strata of her skin, the nurse like an archaeologist, scrubbing the layers away.

They say the body starts dying as soon as you reach thirty. That we all live in various states of decay. In the shower, the water is two degrees too hot. You know what I'm saying when I hand you the sponge. You take your time. I pay attention to the motion of your hands as they follow the muscles along my shoulders. To the sounds of your breath beneath the curtain of water. I close my eyes. I bend my head in prayer.

John Whittier Treat

Nearly

Nearly twenty-five years, still one day, since then
the time when we stood across cold hewn rooms and looked
past what I had wanted (still want) just to see,
I mean steal, that journey of limb and halved-moon curves of
buttock. Now, stacked high above some place far from there,
a room with hot Saint Peter's light cast through shutters onto a
    chair
where lay the quick discard of cotton, perfumed damp torn yours,
limbs yes, buttocks yes, youth no: the force of memories
manufactured if not maintained. Was the motion of a body
ever so sure and feeble? The hurling object knows Newton's Law.
Don't talk, be quiet. Cupping your hand across my mouth,
some things have to close in order to make more room
for others. My body now: a quarter-century of a place where
I had stopped in wait for all that was coming my way, and it has.
Old things made useful again, so go further and be sure to stay
This is that slap of pain and promise of proof for what was not
    love, but nearly;
We've learned in time that what our blood shares makes us special:
then, now, forever

Benjamin Watts

The Pindrop

I ask for somewhere quiet,
so you take me to a bar
on the other side of town
where everyone whispers and hisses
their disobedience.

The drinks are served without ice;
it clinks.
And whenever a train passes by underneath
the bartender presses herself to the wall
to keep the bottles from shaking.

Near the window there's a spot
where the softest twinkling of jazz
has worn great grooves in the floor
from people scooting the chairs
closer together to hear the piano.

It is here, in this stillness
between your swallows and sips
that I decide to love you.
Winking a silent toast,
you lift the glass to your lips
and slurp just a little too loudly.

A man glaring from the corner
sucks his teeth in disapproval.
Instant apology widens in your eyes
and you set the drink down so quickly

on the table it squeaks with a canorous ting.

I giggle, then regret it immediately
when a woman seated at the bar
whips around with such venom and speed
her neck cracks like stalks of celery
being snapped in half.

She stifles a wail with her hand,
knocking over her wine.
Riesling spills to the floor
in a waterfall of broken glass
as the bartender gapes.

With the tenderest, most pleading fingers
you airlift me out of my chair
by the crook of my arm
and whirl me towards the exit,
laughter steaming on your cheeks.

On the street it buckles our knees,
pouring out of us like molten glee.
Between shrieks and breathless,
volcanic howls you sear me
with a smiley, wet-eyed kiss.

Yellow Rose

Worn-out man holding in his hands
his bike and his helmeted head, a slice of pizza
folded up in a paper plate drips
grease onto the floor

He tosses soft stares across the aisle
with menace or longing
at a gay couple younger than god (prettier too)
playing mahjong on their phone and

the long-stemmed yellow rose bobbing between them
Backlit by a halo of setting sun their ears glow pink
Do these flushed angelic lovers know
that yellow is for apologies

Max Wenzel

I'm Intolerable at The Phillips Collection
You are golden, First
Kierkegaard;
nude & young
& shining & I
take your portrait
against a wall of portraits—
nudes and caricatures, kid
in a denim jacket, dutch
self-portrait, also
charcoal on paper, also
lithograph on Arches
paper—in this old mansion.
Once I took a picture
of a kid taking a picture on
his cellphone standing
in front of the giant *La Grande*
Jatte which I think
was on loan from Chicago, where
it's been since the MoMa
let it go back when Frank
O'Hara was still around & Seurat's
sketches for the piece
were on display & I
who am I kidding? All my
pretense of class
& liquor is dropping like
pesticides. In tidal pools
I'm catching a glimpse
of all the metal
admission clips
I didn't keep because
of all the time I spend looking

144

up at cathedral chandeliers & you
are reshaping my vision,
started

Viscous

My best friend's kids can all fry an egg
much better than I can. I'm teaching
myself this morning, sort of swirling
three eggs around in the lard. I find
the sunlight instructive. It dials
across rented wood floors. I try heat
on low, spoon some of the hot oil
over the already slick tops. As a child,
I could never have dreamed of sunny-
side-up and the almost adult ooze
of it all. Now I can't get enough
of the viscous.   A decoy bird
is captured first, and tethered
by the ankle to a limb. A glue made
from mistletoe is wrapped around
the limb like gum around a pencil
or finger. The decoy calls out.
Another bird lands nearby.
It entangles itself in the birdlime.
          The birds outside the kitchen
window are freer. They hop across
branches in the willow. I slide the eggs,
glistening and unbroken onto a plate.
Half an avocado lies open by the sink.
I slice it on top and crack some salt,
some pepper, over it. I hear a man's
naked feet slap across the tile. Last night
I told him what to do. This morning he'll
have coffee. Last night his wedding band
shone in the dim light. I'm glad
he didn't leave it at home, or set it on
my nightstand, but I covered his mouth
when his pleasure got too loud.

The grinder burrs before I take
my first bite: there's no way my parents
could have prepared me for this.

On Sharing the Refrigerator with My Roommates, Revision, and the Suicide Note I Keep on Writing

The girls want all our things
on separate shelves.

I want it all to mix together
until I forget whose olives these are

or that I bought them on some night some
bad thing happened.

Here I'm calling them "the girls" to make them
mad and to kick the can of this "joke"
down the road a little,
a joke about me being misogynist,

which isn't funny.

Mom used to always say "the girls" —

I'm going out with the girls to play bingo—
I told the girls at work how proud I am of you.
Us girls like to dress up once in a while.

used to call her friends who were women
her "girlfriends."

My roommates are women not girls
and what does that matter anyway?

I guess I'm just mad about how much time
I spend alone in the house,

or how last night I had to close the door

to let in a gentleman caller
and someone had to bang around the kitchen
with their boyfriend,
cook something that smells like onions.

I think it's just pizza, though,

because I saw it on one of the shelves.
I don't know whose shelf it is:
I just know it's not mine.

If they ever hear this poem, which is
unlikely, or if this poem ever gets
published, which is even more unlikely,

they'll laugh I guess.

But these days writing every poem
feels like writing a suicide note,

like in this way that I feel that I must
get everything down right now,
because I'm not going to have a chance to revise later.

Revision is a luxury time doesn't always afford us.

If I could, I'd go back
and unwrite that poem about my mom
where I'm at mad her
about what she meant when she said
there's some news she just doesn't want to hear:

in my mind she doesn't want to hear that I have a boyfriend
(I don't have a boyfriend)
or she doesn't want to hear that I have AIDS
(I haven't tested positive).

If I knew she'd only be around for a few
more years I think I'd revise, too,
ever telling her and Dad that I was gay
or I'd like to tell them some truth I didn't know yet:

a forward truth.

But I don't know what the forward truth is:

maybe that I'm queer

maybe that everyone's queer
and it doesn't even matter.

Why'd I want to tell them anyway?

I guess I wouldn't revise any of these things,

don't want to entertain these revisions,
even if revision is a luxury.

This poem, too, is a luxury,

but it feels as vital as a suicide note,

or a refrigerator note:

I left cold brew in the fridge;
it's fair game.

I left a jar of olives;
I don't know
whose it is.

2021 Contributors' Notes

Ezra Adamo is a high school senior from New Orleans in a certificate of artistry program for creative writing and a PLTW biomedical program; although he hasn't done much yet, he hopes to continue attempts at writing and maybe study English when in college. He drinks too much coffee, reads, and does jigsaw puzzles.

Ken Anderson's novel *Someone Bought the House on the Island* was a finalist in the Independent Publisher Book Awards. A stage adaptation won the Saints and Sinners Playwriting Contest and premiered May 2, 2008, at the Marigny Theater in New Orleans. His novel *Sea Change: An Example of the Pleasure Principle* was a finalist for the Ferro-Grumley Award. *The Statue of Pan* (screenplay) is an Official Selection at the LGBTQ Unbordered International Film Festival.

Danielle Bero was born in Queens to hippie parents, given a dose of Shel Silverstein, Tupac, jazz and classic rock. Bero is a Posse scholar, taught in Indonesia on a Fulbright, and co-founded a school for students in foster care. She holds a master's in English Education, Educational Leadership and completed her MFA at the University of San Francisco. She won slams at Nuyorican Poets Café, Bowery Poetry Club and Ubud Writers festival. Bero is a Jack Straw Fellow and is published in Divine Feminist and Aunt Flo Anthologies as well as Lavender Review, Quiet Lightning, Juked and elsewhere.

Steven Cordova's collection of poetry, *Long Distance*, was published by Bilingual Review Press in 2010. His poems are forthcoming in *New Orleans Review,* and have appeared in *Bellevue Literary Review, Callaloo, The Notre Dame Review* and *Los Angeles Review.* From San Antonio, TX, he lives in Brooklyn, New York.

Dante Fuoco is a genderqueer poet, performer, playwright, and video artist based in Brooklyn. His poetry appears in *Ovenbird, Ex-*

position Review, and *KGB Bar Lit,* among other publications. Her latest solo show, *no! i be seal,* was recently staged Off-off-Broadway. A nationally recognized educator, he manages restorative justice and arts programs for a Bronx non-profit. She also coaches an adult LGBTQIA+ swim team in the city.

Stephanie Glazier's poems and critical prose have appeared in the *Alaska and Michigan Quarterly Reviews, Iraq Literary Review,* and in *Reading and Writing Experimental Texts: Critical Innovations.* Her manuscript *Of Fish & Country* was a finalist in the 2020 Perugia Press Prize. Glazier has been a Lambda Literary Fellow, is a Room Project member, holds an MFA from Antioch University LA and serves as the poetry editor for Gertrude Press. She lives and works in Detroit, Michigan.

T.S. Leonard is the author of the poetry chapbooks *Reverse Cowboy* and *The Year in Loss & Faggotry.* A writer and performer, Leonard's work includes the audio project *Even Still They Shook,* short fiction published in Frontera and Buckman Journal, and shouting obscenities in the punk band Soft Butch. A proud after-school art teacher, Leonard still believes in the future.

A native of Berlin, **Helena Lipstadt** lives in Los Angeles and Blue Hill, Maine. Lipstadt is the author of two chapbooks, *Leave Me Signs* and *If My Heart Were A Desert.* Her work has been supported by residencies at WUJS Arts Project, Arad, Israel and Borderland Foundation, Sejny, Poland. Lipstadt, a finalist for Wren Poetry Prize and New Rivers Press 'Many Voices Project', hand built her home in Maine.

Freesia McKee is a poet, micro-memoirist, book reviewer, and teacher. Her words have appeared in *Painted Bride Quarterly, CALYX, Gertrude, So to Speak, Nimrod, GO Magazine,* and the *Ms. Magazine Blog.* Headmistress Press published her poetry chapbook *How Distant the City* in 2018. Find Freesia on Twitter (@freesiamckee) or at FreesiaMcKee.com.

Charlotte O'Brien is a queer writer living in Oakland, California. She graduated from Pacific University's MFA program in 2013 with a concentration in poetry and nonfiction. She has essays and interviews most recently published in The Rumpus, Mutha Magazine, and The Manifest-Station. Her poems, most recently appeared in Reed Magazine, Sheena Na Gig, Epiphany and Catamaran. 'Bones of Flight' was a semifinalist for the Catamaran Poetry Prize. You can find out more about her work at www.charlotteobrien.org

Steven Riel is the author of one full-length collection of poetry (*Fellow Odd Fellow*), with another forthcoming from Lily Poetry Review Books in spring 2021. His most recent chapbook *Postcard from P-town* was published as runner-up for the inaugural Robin Becker Chapbook Prize. His poems have appeared in several anthologies and numerous periodicals, including *The Minnesota Review* and *International Poetry Review*. He serves as editor-in-chief of the Franco-American literary e-journal *Résonance*.

Jessica Sampley is the author of *Tuscaloosa to Tupelo* (MSRP, 2007). Her poems have also appeared in *Birmingham Arts Journal, Kakalak,* and *Indy Weekly*. Jessica grew up in Arley, Alabama. She now lives in Bon Secour, Alabama, with her beautiful wife, Malinda, her elderly mother, Celia; their son, Carson; and their furbabies. Jessica coaches volleyball, sponsors the Equality Club, and serves as the Career Academies Coordinator at Gulf Shores City Schools.

Samantha Tetangco is a queer poet of color whose writing has appeared in dozens of literary magazines, most notably *The Sun, Tri-Quarterly, Puerto del Sol, Cimarron Review,* and others. She has served as editor-in-chief for *Blue Mesa Review,* president of the AWP LGBTQ Writer›s Caucus, and was recently an artist-in-residence at The Studios at MassMOCA. Sam is the Associate Director of Writing at the University of California Merced.

John Whittier Treat was born in New Haven and moved to Seattle in 1983. His poem "When Whitman Met Whittier" appeared in *Lovejets: Queer Male Poets on 200 Years of Whitman*, edited by Raymond Luczak; and his "Smallpox Came to the Northwest in 1770" is included in *Washington 129*, an anthology of Washington State poets edited by Tod Marshall. His new novel, *First Consonants*, is about a stutterer who saves the world. www.johnwhittiertreat.com

Benjamin Watts is a poet and performer living in Brooklyn, New York. His writing explores queerness, family, identity, and the inescapability of his midwestern roots. In his free time, he also moonlights as a tarot card reader. His work is forthcoming in *Revolute*.

Mat Wenzel has 37 stamps in his National Parks Passport, collects squished pennies, and writes poetry and zines. He was a 2015 Lambda Literary Fellow, and his work has appeared in *Homology Lit*, *Crab Fat Magazine*, *Glitterwolf Magazine*, and other journals online and in print. Mat currently teaches at Florida State University.

Our Editors

Paul J. Willis has over 26 years of experience in nonprofit management. He earned a B.S. degree in Psychology and a M.S. degree in Communication. He started his administrative work in 1992 as the co-director of the Holos Foundation in Minneapolis. The Foundation operated an alternative high school program for at-risk youth. Willis has been the executive director of the Tennessee Williams & New Orleans Literary Festival since 2004. He is the founder of the Saints and Sinners Literary Festival (established in 2003). Willis received the Publishing Triangle Award for Leadership (2019). This nationally recognized award is for service to the LGBTQ literary community and was presented at The New School in New York City.

Brad Richard is the author of four poetry collections, most recently *Parasite Kingdom* (The Word Works, 2018), winner of the Tenth Gate Prize. He has taught creative writing at the New Orleans Center for Creative Arts and Lusher Charter School (whose creative writing program he founded and directed), and for New Orleans Writers Workshop and the *Kenyon Review* Writers Workshop for Teachers. He is also imprint editor of the Hilary Tham Capital Collection from The Word Works. 2015 Louisiana Artist of the Year and recipient of fellowships from the Surdna Foundation and the Louisiana Division of the Arts, he lives and writes in New Orleans. More at bradrichard.org.

Our Finalist Judges

Julie R. Enszer, PhD, 2022 Judge, is the author of four poetry collections, including *Avowed*, and the editor of *OutWrite: The Speeches that Shaped LGBTQ Literary Culture*, *Fire-Rimmed Eden: Selected Poems by Lynn Lonidier*, *The Complete Works of Pat Parker*, and *Sister Love: The Letters of Audre Lorde and Pat Parker 1974-1989*. Enszer edits and publishes *Sinister Wisdom*, a multicultural lesbian literary and art journal.

Jewelle Gomez, 2021 Judge, (Cabo Verdean/Wampanoag/Ioway) (she/her), is a novelist, poet, and playwright. Her eight books include three collections of poetry and the first Black lesbian-vampire novel, *The Gilda Stories*. In print for 30 years, it was recently optioned by Cheryl Dunye (*Lovecraft Country*) for a TV mini-series. Her work has appeared in numerous anthologies including, *Red Indian Road West, Dark Matter: A Century of Speculative Fiction from the African Diaspora, Oxford Treasury of Love Stories*, and *Tending the Fire*. Her plays *Waiting for Giovanni* and *Leaving the Blues* were produced in San Francisco and New York City.

Our Cover Artist

Timothy Cummings, represented by Catharine Clark Gallery in San Francisco and Nancy Hoffman Gallery in New York, journeyed to a French Quarter pied-à-terre over-looking Armstrong Park in the Fall of 2017 as part of a My Good Judy Residency. The My Good Judy Foundation provides residencies for artists seeking to produce a body of work or performance in New Orleans that address culture making from an LGBTQ perspective. The residency was established to also honor the work of author and activist Judy Grahn. The subjects of Cummings' work are often children and adolescents struggling with issues of sexuality and sexual orientation in an adult world. In 2013, he was an artist-in-residence and subject of a solo exhibition at Transarte in Sao Paulo, Brazil. His paintings are also part of the collections of Whoopi Goldberg in Los Angeles, CA and Tomaso Bracco and Sara Davis in Milan, Italy.

Timothy enjoyed his time in New Orleans where he received inspiration from the spirits of his favorite writers Tennessee Williams and Truman Capote. "They shaped my early adolescence. They offer a magical telling of the spirit of this place. The darkness and humor of life and the queer Southern aesthetic shows up in my work as well. Williams' "garrulous grotesque," replacing the bleak mundane of the world with a lush queer poetic eye for the shadows is part of my focus," Cummings said. He graciously created an original painting of Tennessee Williams to be used as the cover art for the COVID-cancelled 2020 Tennessee Williams & New Orleans Literary Festival. We're proud to use his artwork for our Festivals, and thank Timothy for the generous donation of this painting to the Festival's fundraising efforts. He resides in a tiny house in Albuquerque, New Mexico. You can see more of Timothy's work at: timothy-cummings.com.

Saints + Sinners Literary Festival

The first Saints and Sinners Literary Festival took place in May of 2003. The event started as a new initiative designed as an innovative way to reach the community with information about HIV/AIDS. It was also formed to bring the LGBT community together to celebrate the literary arts. Literature has long nurtured hope and inspiration, and has provided an avenue of understanding. A steady stream of LGBT novels, short stories, poems, plays, and non-fiction works has served to awaken lesbians, gay men, bisexuals, and transgendered persons to the existence of others like them; to trace the outlines of a shared culture; and to bring the outside world into the emotional passages of LGBTQ life.

After the Stonewall Riots in New York City, gay literature finally came "out of the closet." In time, noted authors such as Dorothy Allison, Michael Cunningham, and Mark Doty (all past *Saints'* participants) were receiving mainstream award recognition for their works. But there are still few opportunities for media attention of gay-themed books, and decreasing publishing options. This Festival helps to ensure that written work from the LGBT community will continue to have an outlet, and that people will have access to books that will help dispel stereotypes, alleviate isolation, and provide resources for personal wellness.

The event has since evolved into a program of the Tennessee Williams & New Orleans Literary Festival made possible by our premier sponsor the John Burton Harter Foundation. The Saints and Sinners LGBTQ Literary Festival works to achieve the following goals:

1. to create an environment for productive networking to ensure increased knowledge and dissemination of LGBTQ literature;
2. to provide an atmosphere for discussion, brainstorming, and the emergence of new ideas;

3. to recognize and honor writers, editors, and publishers who broke new ground and made it possible for LGBTQ books to reach an audience; and

4. to provide a forum for authors, editors, and publishers to talk about their work for the benefit of emerging writers, and for the enjoyment of readers of LGBTQ literature.

Saints and Sinners is an annual celebration that takes place in the heart of the French Quarter of New Orleans each spring. The Festival includes writing workshops, readings, panel discussions, literary walking tours, and a variety of special events. We also aim to inspire the written word through our short fiction contest, and our annual Saints and Sinners Emerging Writer Award sponsored by Rob Byrnes. Each year we induct individuals to our Saints and Sinners Hall of Fame. The Hall of Fame is intended to recognize people for their dedication to LGBTQ literature. Selected members have shown their passion for our literary community through various avenues including writing, promotion, publishing, editing, teaching, bookselling, and volunteerism.

Past year's inductees into the Saints and Sinners Literary Hall of Fame include: Dorothy Allison, Carol Anshaw, Ann Bannon, Lucy Jane Bledsoe, Maureen Brady, Jericho Brown, Rob Byrnes, Patrick Califia, Louis Flint Ceci, Bernard Cooper, Timothy Cummings, Jameson Currier, Brenda Currin, Mark Doty, Mark Drake, Jim Duggins, Elana Dykewomon, Amie M. Evans, Otis Fennell, Michael Thomas Ford, Katherine V. Forrest, Nancy Garden, Jewelle Gomez, Jim Grimsley, Tara Hardy, Ellen Hart, Greg Herren, Kenneth Holditch, Andrew Holleran, Candice Huber, Fay Jacobs, G. Winston James, Saeed Jones, Raphael Kadushin, Michele Karlsberg, Judith Katz, Moises Kaufman, Irena Klepfisz, Joan Larkin, Susan Larson, Lee Lynch, Jeff Mann, William J. Mann, Marianne K. Martin, Paula Martinac, Stephen McCauley, Val McDermid, Mark Merlis, Tim Miller, Rip & Marsha Naquin-Delain, Michael Nava, Achy Obejas, Felice Picano, Radclyffe, J.M. Redmann, David Rosen, Carol Rosenfeld, Steven Saylor, Carol Seajay, Martin Sherman, Kelly Smith, Jack Sullivan, Carsen Taite, Cecilia Tan, Noel Twilbeck, Jr., Patricia Nell

Warren, Jess Wells, Don Weise, Edmund White, and Paul J. Willis.

For more information about the Saints and Sinners Literary Festival including sponsorship opportunities and our Archangel Membership Program, visit: www.sasfest.org. Be sure to sign up for our e-newsletter for updates for future programs. We hope you will join other writers and bibliophiles for a weekend of literary revelry not to be missed!

"Saints & Sinners is hands down one of the best places to go to revive a writer's spirit. Imagine a gathering in which you can lean into conversations with some of the best writers and editors and agents in the country, all of them speaking frankly and passionately about the books, stories and people they love and hate and want most to record in some indelible way. Imagine a community that tells you truthfully what is happening with writing and publishing in the world you most want to reach. Imagine the flirting, the arguing, the teasing and praising and exchanging of not just vital information, but the whole spirit of queer arts and creating. Then imagine it all taking place on the sultry streets of New Orleans' French Quarter. That's Saints & Sinners—the best wellspring of inspiration and enthusiasm you are going to find. Go there."

—Dorothy Allison, National Book Award finalist
for *Bastard Out of Carolina*, and author
of the critically acclaimed novel *Cavedweller*.

CPSIA information can be obtained
at www.ICGtesting.com
Printed in the USA
BVHW080213070322
630719BV00002B/7